A Short History of the Hungarian Communist Party

A Short History of the Hungarian Communist Party
Miklós Molnár

In spite of its small size, the Hungarian Communist party (HCP), founded in the fall of 1918, has played an important role both in Hungary's national history and in the international communist movement. Hungary, which was the only soviet republic other than the ephemeral Bavarian soviet republic to exist outside the USSR, lasted five months during the critical period of the Paris Peace Conference. The "veterans" of the Hungarian soviet republic, like Béla Kun, Georg Lukács, and Eugen Varga, later held important posts in the Comintern and in the international Communist press. In the Stalinist era, the HCP distinguished itself by excessive zeal in the application of "integral Stalinism" in foreign policy (e.g., anti-Titoism), the economy, and political life (e.g., the Rajk and Kádár trials). However, the 1956 revolution was engineered by the revisionist communist intelligentsia and by such revisionist party leaders as Imre Nagy. Finally, in spite of its repressive role after the revolution, in the 1970s under János Kádár the HCP introduced a new system of "liberalism" and economic reform.

This volume was written on the basis of official party publications, memoirs, the contemporary press, and research conducted in Hungarian, Austrian, French, and Italian archives.

Miklós Molnár is professor of the history of international relations and of contemporary history at the Graduate Institute of International Studies (GIIS), Geneva, and at Lausanne University. Dr. Molnár studied in Budapest, where he was editor-in-chief of *Iradalmi Ujsag,* and received his Ph.D. from the GIIS. Among his books are *Le Déclin de la Première Internationale* and *A History of the Hungarian Revolution.*

A Short History of the Hungarian Communist Party

Miklós Molnár

Westview Press • Boulder, Colorado

Dawson • Folkestone, England

This volume is included in Westview's Special Studies on the Soviet Union and Eastern Europe.

Published in 1978 in the United States of America by
  Westview Press, Inc.
  5500 Central Avenue
  Boulder, Colorado 80301
  Frederick A. Praeger, Publisher and Editorial Director

Published in 1978 in Great Britain by
  Wm. Dawson and Sons, Ltd.
  Cannon House
  Folkestone
  Kent CP19 5EE

Library of Congress Number: 77-27898
ISBN (U.S.): 0-89158-332-7
ISBN (U.K.): 07129-0872-2
Printed and bound in the United States of America

Contents

1. History

Origins

There is no authentic, accessible historical evidence that allows us to establish precisely the dates, places, and circumstances of the foundation of the Hungarian Communist party (HCP).[1] According to a vast collection of documents published in 1956 by the Institute for Party History, such evidence was not available at that time.[2] Subsequent publications do not fill this gap either. Therefore, various works either differ about the dates and places of the first, founding meeting of the HCP, or they avoid providing detailed information about it. This is particularly true of the *Munkásmozgalomtörténeti Lexikon* [Historical dictionary of the workers' movement] (1972),[3] as well as of a recent collective historical study (1968) dedicated to the history of the HCP's organization.[4]

In any case, two separate initiatives lie at the origin of the HCP: one taken by socialist groups, both revolutionary and leftist, in Hungary, the other by Hungarian prisoners of war in Russia who had adhered to the revolution and the Bolshevik party. As early as October 1918, the socialist groups in Hungary were considering the formation of either a communist circle (Karl Marx Circle or Ervin Szabó Circle) or a revolutionary socialist party separate from the Social Democratic party (SDP). On November 15, 1918, with the foundation of this party in mind, they organized a meeting in a printer's shop at 12 József Square.[5] According to available sources, however, the party was not as yet founded on this date. The 1956 collection of documents gives November 20 as the date of its foundation. The Hungarian historian György Milei, a specialist on this question, has enumerated all the accessible sources and dates mentioned therein—November 17, 21, 22, 24, and 28. After comparing the evidence, he concluded that the most likely date is November 24 and that the most likely location is a private apartment on Városmajor Street in a residential neighborhood on the right bank of the Danube.[6] It was there, in fact, that Béla Kun and his friends, having arrived from Moscow on November 19, met with their comrades of the socialist left in order to found the Hungarian Communist party. However, this does not rule out the possibility that such an initiative had been taken even before their arrival, probably by János Hirossik.

Be that as it may, the communists who came from Russia played a major role in the actual establishment of the HCP, if only by reason of the prestige that surrounded the Russian Bolshevik party, its leader Lenin, and its principles of revolutionary organization, to which the group from Russia laid claim.

The origin of this group, which was led by Béla Kun, goes back to 1917. In several prison camps in Russia, soldiers supported the revolution, especially in Siberia. In Omsk, the Hungarian Károly Ligeti established and presided over the International Socialist (later Communist) Party of Prisoners of War. Still in Omsk, Ligeti published the Hungarian newspaper *Forradalom* [Revolution]. In the meantime, several other communist groups were formed, notably in Tomsk, Ivanovo, Krasnoiarsk, Tver, and Petrograd. On March 24, 1918, a central organization was founded in Moscow—it united the communist prisoners under the name of Hungarian Group of the Communist Party (Bolshevik) of Russia. This group published the biweekly *Szociális Forradalom* [Social revolution] as well as a number of propaganda pamphlets, written chiefly by Béla Kun, Tibor Szamuely, and Károly Vántus. It belonged to the International Federation of Foreign Groups of the Communist Party (Bolshevik) of Russia, founded in May under the chairmanship of Kun, and it had its headquarters at the Hotel Dresden in Moscow. At the end of 1918, it had about 90 members in Moscow and 150-170 in several other cities and fighting units of the Red Army. According to another version, the group had 350-370 members: among others, 130 in Russia, 25 in the Ukraine, and about 300 returnees in Hungary. We shall come back to these 300.[7]

It is important to note that this federation, which united the Hungarian, Rumanian, Yugoslav, Czechoslovak, and German groups (to which were soon added the Finnish, French, Bulgarian, and Anglo-American groups), operated under the direction of the Central Committee of the Communist party (Bolshevik) through the intermediary of its Hungarian, Rumanian, and other sections created within the Central Committee in March 1918. The Federation of Foreign Groups was to enroll all foreigners who were members of the Bolshevik party and to "unite them in the Third International."[8] In addition, it was directly responsible for propaganda and organization among all prisoners of war as well as for the troops who fought against the Czechoslovak Legion.[9] Lastly, it had under its direction the German and Austro-Hungarian councils of prisoners of war, which had come into being in November 1918, after the collapse of the Reich and the Dual Monarchy. As a result, the Hungarian group found itself part of a wide network, whose objectives were: (1) the organization of combat units for the Russian revolution; (2) propaganda and organizational work with a view toward revolutions in Germany and in the former Austria-Hungary; and (3) the organization of embryonic communist parties to be joined with the Third International, which itself was in the process of formation. All these activities fell under the direction of the Central Committee of the Bolshevik party, where Béla Kun, according to many indications, enjoyed a rather exceptional role and prestige. This situation undoubtedly explains the particularly close relationship between, on the one hand, the leading circles in Moscow, including Lenin himself, and, on the other hand, the future Soviet Republic of Hungary. Likewise, it sheds light on the role played by the group of Hungarian émigrés in Moscow after the collapse of the dictatorship in Hungary.

Established then on March 24, 1918, the Hungarian Group of the Communist Party (Bolshevik) of Russia, in addition to its propaganda and organizational work, formed an "agitator school," which trained 102 "agitator-propagandists" in five special courses. This number does not include those who received their training in Omsk from Ligeti's group and probably some others as well. According to the Hungarian historian Dr. Tibor Szamuely, 745 Hungarian prisoners attended the different agitator schools. According to a report of the Hungarian Group, 20 graduates from the Moscow school went to Hungary in October 1918, and 80 more in November 1918, in addition to "100-120 regular soldiers of the party."[10]

In the meantime, several meetings took place in Russia for the purpose of forming the Hungarian Communist party. Already on July 10, 1918, it had been decided to convene those Hungarian communists of Russia who were ready to go to Hungary in order to establish the party. At another meeting, held on August 25, Tibor Szamuely reported on his discussion with Lenin, who had inquired about the Hungarian Social Democratic party to learn whether cooperation between communists and social democrats would be possible. On October 25, Kun laid down the principles that were to preside over the formation of a Hungarian Communist party of the Bolshevik type. Finally, on November 4, the group of Austro-Hungarian communists of the Bolshevik party founded, still at the Hotel Dresden, the Communist party of Hungary, the "Hungarian Section of the International Communist Party." They announced their intention to follow the direction of the Central Committee of the Bolshevik party until the Third International was established. The new party ordered its members to return to Hungary with the least possible delay. It elected a Provisional Central Committee, which was composed of Károly Vántus, Béla Kun, Ernö Pór, Hariton Beszkarid, Emil Bozdogh, Mátyás Kovács, Mátyás Krisják, Iván Matuzovits, and Ferenc Drobnik.[11]

The following day, Kun and several other members of the group set out for Hungary, where they arrived by mid-November. According to the report of the Hungarian Communist Group mentioned above, other "agitators," sent from Moscow as early as October, were already there. Still others arrived later, either from Russia or from other countries. For example, Tibor Szamuely had been sent on a mission to Switzerland and to the Spartacus League in Berlin and had stayed there until January 1919. Under these circumstances it is difficult to state accurately the total number of communists who came from Russia or to list the leading members who participated in the foundation of the CP in Hungary. For the former, the report of the Communist Group of Moscow seems to be the only available source. But it is not known whether the hundred "agitators" mentioned in the December report include the group of militants dispatched to Budapest in mid-November and after. Nevertheless, the relatively limited number of Hungarian communists organized in the group at the end of 1918 and the beginning of 1919 leads one to believe that no more than 250-300 agents arrived in Hungary—the more so since a nucleus stayed in Russia in order to take care of former Hungarian prisoners (almost half a million), both those who were part of the Red Army and those who were not. This nucleus grew constantly, if one judges by the 3,400 members registered at the Central Office of the seventy-six Hungarian communist groups in Russia.

These thousands of communists, who did not participate in party activities during the existence of the Republic of the Councils of Hungary, were either sent on a clandestine mission to Hungary in the second half of 1920 and in 1921, or else settled in Russia.

According to the most recent work on the question, the first Central Committee (elected by the HCP's founding meeting [or meetings] included the following members of the Moscow group: Béla Kun, Ferenc Jancsik, Ernö Pór, József Rabinovics, Ernö Seidler, Károly Vántus, as well as Tibor Szamuely after his return.[12] Hence, of the nine members of the Provisional Central Committee established in Moscow on November 4, one finds again three: Kun, Pór, and Seidler.

According to the same work, the other two constituent groups were represented as follows: Béla Vágó, Ede Chlepko, Rezsö Fiedler, János Hirossik, Jenö László, László Rudas, and Béla Szántó of the leftist social democrats who had broken away from their former party; and finally, Otto Korvin and József Mikulin of the Revolutionary Socialists.

According to other works, other leaders were Ferenc Münnich, Frigyes Karikás, Mátyás Rákosi, Sándor Kellner, and Gyula Alpári—all of whom, however, were not among the original "founders." Certain leftist leaders of the Republic of the Councils and future communists such as Jenö Varga, Jenö Landler, and others still remained members of the Social Democratic party.

The Moscow group, even if it played a very important role in organizing the new party, would undoubtedly not have been able to win acceptance for communist principles without the help of the other two constituent groups. Of these, the Revolutionary Socialists actually came from two main sources. One was the left wing of the Galileo Circle, which as early as 1908 had united the intelligentsia and radical student groups. Karl Polányi, who received international recognition for his writings composed in exile in

Germany, in England after 1933, and finally in the United States, was among the leaders of this intellectual movement, along with the great poet Endre Ady and many future communists, such as Otto Korvin and Imre Sallai. Also very close to the Galileo Circle was another group centered around Ervin Szabó, which likewise joined the revolutionary socialist movement. More than radical, Ervin Szabó and his followers were anarcho-syndicalists. It was from this position that Szábo, since the early years of the century, had been criticizing German as well as Hungarian social democracy. Theorist and sociologist, Szabó, through his work and his personality, left his mark not only on his group but on a great part of the left intelligentsia. An antimilitarist, Szabó pursued his revolutionary propaganda against the war, especially from 1917. After his death in September 1918, several of his followers drifted toward communism, particularly József Révai, in addition to those already mentioned. Of the left social democrats who joined the HCP from the very first, János Hirossik seems to have played the most important political role. Close to Gyula Alpári, he was, from 1910, one of the leaders of the left opposition within his party, which eventually expelled him in 1912. The routes the others took were often different, but their profound motivation was the same, namely, dissatisfaction with the Social Democratic party, which they regarded as becoming more and more bourgeois and revisionist, as well as with the Second International, paralyzed by the fact that its more important parties had approved the war effort in their respective countries and had even entered the governments of the Union Sacrée. The October revolution in Russia and the revolutionary, antimilitary, and internationalist politics of the Bolsheviks could only deepen the divergences between those leftist elements and the established socialist parties.

Certainly, all these leftist groups together were only an extremely small minority of the socialist elite, or even of the radical elite. According to Vilmos Böhm, one of the social democratic leaders, they represented only a handful of persons who had long been "dissatisfied for personal reasons" and who had left the party or had been expelled.[13] Whatever their personal reasons, however, there were also profound political and ideological factors and, the decisive element, the radicalizing effect of the situation itself. Radicalization had been started by the war, widened by the revolution in Russia, and it gained momentum in dramatic fashion after the military defeat, the dissolution of the Austro-Hungarian army, and the disintegration of the Dual Monarchy. If the great and prestigious Social Democratic party was itself driven to merge in March 1919 with the HCP, which had been founded hardly four months before, it was because the political crisis in the country had become more and more serious.

It was in this crisis that the HCP was founded and quickly rose to power. This is not the place to analyze this crisis itself; our object is merely to point out the elements that may throw light on the rise of the HCP.

The military collapse produced in Hungary not only an economic emergency, but also a serious political crisis. Two parties of the democratic opposition, the Independence party headed by Count Mihály Károlyi and the National Radical Bourgeois party, together with the Social Democratic party decided on October 15, 1918, to form a Hungarian National Council. Three days later, the troubles that had been endemic for more than a month took on revolutionary proportions. First, there was a mass demonstration in Budapest on the twenty-eighth; then, on the evening of the thirtieth, revolution broke out. The Soldiers' Council, created the day before, arrested the commanding general of Budapest, but even without this, no unit would have obeyed him any longer. The army was in complete disarray; what remained of it placed itself at the disposal of the National Council, offering it control over the capital on the following day.

Count Károlyi formed a coalition government under the aegis of the National Council. But immediately popular unrest, particularly among the workers, resumed in order to push the government to proclaim the republic. Finally, on November 13, King Charles of Habsburg signed, in pencil, a document surrendering power, and on the sixteenth, in front of a crowd estimated at 200,000 people, Count Károlyi announced the advent of the first Hungarian republic.[14]

Contrary to what numerous historical works erroneously affirm, no such decision had ever been taken during the Hungarian Revolution and the War of Independence of 1848-1849. Kossuth contented himself with proclaiming the dethronement of the Habsburgs, but he did not establish a republic. Nevertheless, the Hungarian Revolution of October-November 1918 was a republican-democratic movement in the spirit of '48 both in style and in substance. This is also true on the political and economic levels. The numerous radical measures that were taken during the five months of the Károlyi administration (which was reorganized several times, particularly in consideration of Károlyi's election to the presidency of the Republic) tended to modernize and democratize the country. For some it was not enough, for others it was far too much. In any case, the heterogeneous composition of the forces in power did not allow the radical transformation of agrarian structures, thus leaving in suspense for a quarter of a century the revendication of the poor peasantry, which made up half the population.

Still, the fact remains that the Democratic Republic did not fail because of domestic problems. It failed because of the international balance of power. Confronted with the nationality movement, which had become the pivotal issue in the reorganization of Central Europe and the Balkans, placed in a difficult position toward the powers of the Entente—especially France—Count Károlyi failed in his foreign policy. Unable to obtain concessions from the great powers, harassed by Czechoslovakia and Rumania (which were eager above all to weaken Hungary), Károlyi saw himself driven into a choice worthy of Corneille: to give in or to resign. After having signed the Armistice of Belgrade, which was already very unfavorable to Hungary, he was called upon to surrender still more vast stretches of territory—as a "neutralized zone"—for the benefit of the neighboring states. This was done also for the purpose of creating a cordon sanitaire around Bolshevik Russia. It was long believed that this represented a relatively autonomous policy on the part of the French general staff, in particular, Marshal General Foch and General Franchet d'Esperey. In reality, Clemenceau's direct instructions to the French commander-in-chief were of the same general nature. Faced with an ultimatum presented on March 20 by the French Lieutenant-Colonel Vyx, the Károlyi administration resigned. On March 21, the two workers' parties, Social Democrats and Communists, united, proclaimed the Republic of the Hungarian Councils, and formed, for the purposes of governing, a "Revolutionary Council of Government."[15]

The HCP in the Republic
of the Councils of Hungary

Owing to the revolution and the republic, and favored by a crisis that radicalized the workers as well as the lower middle classes, the HCP undoubtedly gained ground during the first months of 1919. According to the sources and the works published by the Institute for Party History of the Central Committee of the HCP, there is no precise information concerning the number of its followers in 1919. There were 10,000 in January, according to the party secretariat at the time. In March, the bill of indictment prepared by the public prosecutor of the Károlyi administration against the communist leaders, who were imprisoned for a few weeks, gave the membership as between 30,000 and 40,000. Compared to the HCP, the Social Democratic party, whose organization was based on the unions, was a much more powerful force. In comparison to 1913, the number of unionized workers had doubled on the eve of the revolution, exceeding 200,000 members. In December, there were already 721,000, not including the newly established agrarian workers' unions. However, this number included the floating mass of those who had adhered to the cause under the influence of the revolutionary climate, even, to mention one or two extreme cases . . . the policemen of a garrison or the members of the lumber and coal merchants' union, who discovered they had a belated socialist vocation.

According to the memoirs of Böhm, the hard-core social democratic nucleus was hardly more than 50,000-60,000 workers. This causes the author, albeit involuntarily, to attribute an indisputable importance to the communist core, still inferior certainly, but organized around the party and not around the unions.[16]

In a climate of crisis and agitation, it is not only the number of supporters that counts. Böhm still affirms that the HCP's propaganda practice of constant outbidding could not help but succeed "in the vast army of unemployed, among the tens of thousands of invalids who lived in atrocious misery, among the hundreds of thousands of demobilized soldiers, demoralized and deprived of their homes. . . . On these masses Béla Kun constructed his whole policy. He aligned against the organized workers who had developed class consciousness the unorganized masses who acted counter to class consciousness."[17]

The HCP, to be sure, judges the situation differently, today as at the time. Communist writers emphasize above all the success of communist infiltration and influence in the factories, the unions, and the social democratic organizations. Tactics of forming communist cells? Certainly. But if these tactics succeeded to a certain extent, it was because the HCP's often demagogic propaganda was suited to the climate of crisis and radicalization, as well as to the shift of the social democratic masses toward the left. As for the unorganized masses, the demobilized troops and disabled soldiers, the unemployed, and even the lumpenproletariat, they were undoubtedly an important clientele for the communists. But

was it not Lenin himself who, as early as 1905, had advocated tactics aimed, in addition to the urban proletariat, at all
the disadvantaged and unhappy elements in society "all
without exception: artisans, the wretchedly poor, beggars,
servants, vagabonds, prostitutes"?[18]

As for the financial resources of the HCP, bourgeois and
social democratic authors have not failed to point out their importance. The funds received from Moscow allowed the HCP
to start newspapers, to print pamphlets, to have working
capital for its organizations and, probably, for other purposes. The coffers of the party were not empty, far from it.
Recently, the historians of the HCP for the first time identi-
fied the origin of these funds:

> The Hungarian CP maintained close relations with the
> Bolshevik Party. A courier service operated between
> Budapest and Moscow. Those who knew the way,
> former prisoners of war from the two countries, car-
> ried out this dangerous and responsible work; they
> assured the transmission of reciprocal messages, par-
> ticularly the information for Lenin on the ripening
> revolutionary situation in Hungary. Through the
> intermediary of couriers, the Bolshevik Party took
> care of the financial needs of the Hungarian CP, thus
> making possible the publication of newspapers, prop-
> aganda documents and pamphlets as well as the pur-
> chase of weapons.[19]

Through all these circumstances, the HCP assumed the
leadership of the movement—which was already launched
before the HCP's own foundation[20]—for the revolution and
the republic of the soviets, for the dictatorship of the proletariat—a program judged to be premature by the Social Democratic party. Numerous demonstrations marked the way of
this second revolution. There were strikes in the cities, where,
besides the Soldiers' Council, the Workers' Council of
Budapest and those of other cities gained more and more importance. In the countryside, the agrarian workers and the

poor peasants attacked the estate system, the legacy of a lingering feudalism. On January 28, the SDP nevertheless was able to exclude the communists from the Workers' Council of Budapest, and a few days later from the unions. Among the large revolutionary mass organizations, only the Soldiers' Council remained linked to the HCP, which, however, maintained its position in the local union organizations.

Held responsible for a fusillade, the HCP leaders and 200 other militants were arrested. Among them were Béla Kun and several other members of the Central Committee of the party and of the Association of the Young Socialists. Therefore, a provisional central committee was formed in order to organize a campaign for the release of the prisoners. In the end, instead of losing its influence, the HCP made gains as a result of this affair. Within the SDP, the left wing, headed by several future communists, such as Landler and Varga, prevailed over the centrists. The prison where the communists were detained became a kind of secret meeting place: the social democrats had come to see the communists and discussed with them the eventuality of seizing power through the unification of the two parties.

After Count Károlyi's resignation, the other social democratic leaders, with a few exceptions, also adhered to this plan of action. On March 21, an official delegation went to the prison to confirm the agreement that was to give birth to the unified Socialist-Communist party and the Republic of the Councils of Hungary.

In accord with this agreement, the new party adopted the name of Socialist Party of Hungary; at the same time it accepted the conditions put forward by the communists concerning its provisional program. Consequently, the new party agreed to the following principles: adhesion to the Third International, alliance with Soviet Russia, nationalization of the means of production, seizure of power by the proletariat, and the Republic of the Councils.

Here is the text of this unique historical document:

The Social Democratic Party of Hungary and the Party of the Communists of Hungary have decided today, in a joint meeting of the party leadership, on the complete union of the two parties.

The name of the new united party, as long as the revolutionary International has not decided on the definitive name of the party, shall be "Socialist Party of Hungary."

The union takes place on the following basis and in such a way that the representatives of the Party of the Communists of Hungary participate equally in the leadership of the party and in political power [*kormányhatalom*]. The party, in the name of the proletariat, immediately assumes complete authority. The dictatorship of the proletariat is exercised by the councils of workers, peasants, and soldiers. For this reason, the project of elections for the national assembly is of course [*természetszerüen*] definitely shelved.

The class army of the proletariat must be created immediately in order to completely disarm the bourgeoisie.

In order to ensure the power of the proletariat as well as for the fight against the imperialism of the Entente, the most complete and most intimate military and spiritual alliance must be concluded with the Russian Soviet government.

Budapest, March 21, 1919.

In the name of the Social Democratic Party of Hungary:

Jenö Landler, Zsigmund Kunfy, Jakab Weltner, József Pogány, József Haubrich.

In the name of the Party of the Communists of Hungary:

Béla Kun, Ferenc Jancsik, Béla Szántó, Béla Vágó, Károly Vántus, Ede Chlepko, Ernö Seidler, József Rabinovits.[21]

After this agreement, the seizure of political power was no longer a problem. The Berinkey administration, which had resigned, took note of it and retreated. The president of the

Republic, Count Károlyi, resigned. Did he resign his post directly, or did he hand over power to the proletariat? The question remains controversial. Károlyi himself sometimes denied that he abandoned the field and relinquished his powers to the socialo-communists; sometimes, during his periods of rapprochement with the latter, he intimated that this had indeed been his intention. Károlyi's unpublished papers are still in the possession of his widow, who, in her own memoirs, confirms the version according to which the famous declaration of March 22 announcing that the president had resigned and "transmitted power to the Hungarian proletariat" was "a proclamation that had appeared under the name of Michel." But she also confirms that Károlyi, even if he had not signed this text, was aware of the impact of his decision, even that he would have wished to persuade the conservatives that in the present situation"one cannot do anything else but support the communists because that means the defense of the country and that one should not and could under no circumstances accept the note of the Entente."[22] The Entente's rejection of Hungary, in any case, was to play an important part in turning the country toward proletarian government at home and toward Soviet Russia abroad. The armies of the latter were approaching via Lvov and Rumania.

Immediately after the unification, the direction of the new party seemed to remain in the hands of the social democratic leaders and their solid and experienced party machine. Since the HCP was dissolved, the communists entered the organizations of the former SDP. On the other hand, within the government (the "Revolutionary Council of Government"), where the communists were in a strong position, a Politburo consisting of five members received the task of defining the politics of the dictatorship of the proletariat until the convocation of a party congress. This gave it a strong influence on the party. As highest executive organ, the revolutionary government thus held the actual reins of power, and the influence of Béla Kun was and remained decisive there. The party congress that assembled on June 12-13 only further strengthened the position of the communists. Five of the thirteen members of the Central Committee came from the former HCP, and one or two others from the socialist left.

Within the party, then, power seemed to be divided between former communists and centrist social democrats, with the socialist left assuming the role of arbiter. This arrangement did not fail to annoy Béla Kun and his comrades, just as they were irked by the presence of moderate elements in the heart of government agencies. On the whole, however, the communists and Béla Kun personally left their mark on the policies of the Republic of the Councils owing to the support of the left socialists and probably to the support of Russia and particularly Lenin.

The latter followed daily the events in Hungary, not only by means of the courier service—which had become more and more difficult by reason of the successive defeats of the Red Army and its greater distance from the Hungarian borders—but chiefly by means of the telegraph. Lenin did not neglect to urge Béla Kun and his comrades to follow the example of the Bolsheviks, especially with regard to the absolute suspicion toward the former social democrats as well as to the use of relentless terror. Indeed, the police apparatus of the dictatorship of the proletariat, set up and directed by the communists independently of the official police, was a valuable power lever for the communists. One heavily armed detachment even sported the name "Terror troops of the Revolutionary Council of Government"; it was also known as the "Lenin boys."[23] Under pressure from the social democrats, the unit was disbanded and, if only partially, integrated into the department of Otto Korvin, head of the political section of the Ministry of the Interior.

Thus the history of the HCP during the 133 days of the dictatorship is inextricable from that of the unified party, which, at its congress in June, took the name of Socialist-Communist Workers' Party of Hungary; and it is inextricable from the history of the Republic of the Councils of Hungary. The extremely complex organization of political power, the frequent changes, the rapid political evolution, and finally the war—all make it impossible to relate this history here.[24]

The revolutionary government first consisted of thirty people's commissars and deputy commissars as well as of five other delegates to the city of Budapest and to the Department of Police and Public Order. A clever distribution of posts allowed the communists, as already pointed out, to keep the decision-making power and, even more, the executive power, in the hands of the party and its allies. The common program based on the March 21 agreement also permitted them to carry out revolutionary measures more bolshevik than socialist in type.

Many leaders of 1919 were to play an important role in the Comintern, in the HCP once it was compelled to go underground, and in postwar Hungary: for example, Béla Kun, Jenö Landler, Jenö Varga, Georg Lukács, Béla Szántó, Mátyás Rákosi, and others.

The bolshevik measures included the nationalization of companies with more than twenty workers and employees, of all banks and financial institutions, of insurance companies, apartment buildings, and wholesale trade. The great fortunes deposited in banks were confiscated, the middle-sized deposits were put under control, as were retail shops. Thus the decrees of the dictatorship of the proletariat hit not only the upper bourgeoisie but also the middle classes. The liberal professions were likewise not spared: lawyers, doctors, and artists were forced to yield to government control and were often limited in their activities, as in the case of the lawyers. Certainly Béla Kun and his companions could not draw on the Soviet experience—the NEP came only in 1921. Moreover, they did not have the time to draw the lessons from their own experiment. Therefore, the excessive expropriations slowed the country's economy, which was already disrupted by the consequences of the war: scarcity of raw materials and food supplies, rationing, and inflation. The Hungarian crown, which was on a par with the Swiss franc before the war, had lost two-thirds of its value—thirty francs against 100 crowns—at the end of 1918 and fell to eighteen francs in April and to eleven in August. The domestic disorder was further compounded by the fact that the government, following the example of Károlyi's administration, circulated so-called white notes instead of the "blue" notes of the monarchy, which only increased the distrust toward its currency. The issuance of new notes began in June, which coincided with the recall of the old notes, but could not restore confidence nor prevent the flight of and speculation on the blue notes.[25]

In a predominantly agrarian country such as Hungary, policies toward the peasants were of utmost importance. With a suitable land reform, the dictatorship acting in the name of the proletariat might perhaps have been able to win the support of the poor peasants and agricultural workers, these "three million beggars," victims of a system of latifundia inherited from feudalism. But instead of redistributing the landed property of the magnates as the Bolsheviks had done, the Hungarian communists gave it to agricultural cooperatives. This "great leap forward" could only disenchant an important political clientele and give rise to insecurity and hostility among the rich and middle peasants.

With penury, insecurity, rising prices, depreciation of money, and unemployment, generous social measures could not remedy the economic troubles. However, there were many measures in behalf of the most disfavored wage earners, the poor, children, women, and still other groups.

The changes that occurred during the four months the regime was in existence did not affect its domestic policy. In fact, despite the dissatisfaction in various segments of the population, the unified party grew constantly: from 800,000 after the unification, the number of the union members, who were automatically integrated into the party, reached one and a half million in August, before the collapse. As for the balance of power in the leading organs, the communists, with the help of the left socialists, were able to maintain slight preponderance. Indeed, neither at the congress of the new party on June 12-13 nor at the National Congress of the Councils on June 14-23 did the social democrats of the center succeed in gaining the upper hand. The new government, the true holder of power, elected at the end of the Congress of the Councils by the new Executive Committee, consisted of nine communist and left socialist members as opposed to six of the center, of whom two were commissars for nationalities and had little influence. At the same time, the leader of the center Zsigmond Kunfi, withdrew from the government, abandoning the field to his main partner and adversary, Béla Kun.

The Congress of the Councils, acting as a constituent assembly, promulgated the new constitution. The constitution also bore the mark of the left majority, acknowledging particularly the principle of the dictatorship of the proletariat. The state also took its definitive name for the five weeks that it was to last: Magyarországi szocialista szövetséges Tanácsköztársaság—that is, Federal Socialist Republic of the Councils of Hungary. The word *Federal* reflects the fact that the Burgenland and sub-Carpathian Ruthenia were still a part of Hungary. But the Constituent Assembly may also have wished to emphasize the soviet character of the government in the sense of self-government. The Republic, according to paragraph two, "is the republic of the workers', peasants', and soldiers' councils."[26] In reality, however, the constitution gave the real power to the central administration, leaving little competence to the local councils, which were, moreover, elected by universal suffrage but on single lists, just as the delegates to the congress had been.

Since the ephemeral Soviet Republic of Hungary was the

only soviet regime in 1919 that consistently tried to establish
the dictatorship of the proletariat in imitation of the Bolsheviks, its short history has given rise to many interpretations.
Despite their initial enthusiasm, the Russian leaders, above all
Lenin, did not hesitate to severely criticize Béla Kun's team
for the errors they made during the 133 days of the republic.
They reproached them mainly for the union between the
Communist party and the Social Democratic party, without
taking into account Kun's essential objection that without
the socialists, the minuscule Communist party not only
would never have come to power, but also that its captive
leaders would not have been able to get out . . . of prison.[27]
Little by little, Kun was forced, reluctantly, to recognize as
an error what he had however regarded as a necessity. In an
article published in 1924 in Moscow, Kun, drawing the conclusions of 1919, summed up the causes for the defeat of the
dictatorship in four points: (1) a strategic retreat in a territory as small as Hungary was impossible; (2) international
circumstances were unfavorable; (3) there was no effective
Communist party; and finally (4) the land reform was unsuc-
cessful. Under point three, coming back to the question of
the unification of the two parties, he recognized that it was
not possible to "correct the error of the unification" because
"the Communist party dissolved in the Social Democratic
party, and the latter dissolved, blended into the workers'
councils and the various institutions of the councils."
"During the dictatorship, there was absolutely no organized
workers' party." He further added that according to many
communists, this was not even necessary. "The councils—
that's all."[28]

Kun's analyses are interesting from different points of
view. More than the confession of a mistake, his self-criticism
is an admission of the inherent weaknesses of the Communist
party, which he himself had founded on the eve of the events
of 1919. To be complete, Kun had only to add another
acknowledgment, the one made by his comrade Jenö Varga,

who, also reflecting on the causes for the failure, went back to its most profound cause: the absence of a revolution. The HCP had not seized power by force. It had received it. Circumstances had created the Republic of the Councils, the proletarian revolution had not.

But likewise the tide of events, more than its own mistakes, led to its fall. Kun was not wrong to put half the blame for the failure of his undertaking on the military situation and international circumstances. He compares, discreetly, to be sure, the disadvantageous conditions of the 1919 dictatorship in Hungary with the favorable situation of 1917, which was "several times pointed out by comrade Lenin as having been one of the factors for the success of the Russian Revolution."[29]

The study of these external factors, diplomatic and military, exceeds the limits of our work. It would take us to the Paris Peace Conference, particularly to the discussions among Wilson, Clemenceau, Lloyd George, and Orlando, that is, the Council of Four, which followed events in Soviet Hungary with great attention.[30] Furthermore, the Big Four were kept well informed about the situation by semiofficial agents, such as Professor Philip Marshall Brown, the president's advisor, or by diplomats at their post or on a mission, such as General Smuts, head of an Entente delegation sent to Budapest. However, all attempts at negotiation (there was even a suggestion to invite Béla Kun to Paris) and at mediation failed— for two closely related reasons. French diplomacy and its head, Stéphen Pichon, were uniformly hostile toward Hungary, both as an enemy state and as a communist regime. It is difficult to know which of the two elements had more weight in the decisions, but in any case French diplomacy wished to see the demise of the Republic of the Councils as quickly as possible—with the help of especially the Rumanian and Czechoslovak armies. At the same time, the cordon sanitaire, so dear to Marshal Foch, was to pass through Hungary; it also facilitated the supply of the necessary support for

Rumania and Czechoslovakia. The French plan of an Entente intervention through these two countries was rejected, but in fact Soviet Hungary had been at war with these two countries since mid-April. Rumanian troops occupied Northeast Hungary up to Debrecen and Szolnok, and Czechoslovak troops were stopped and then driven back by the Hungarian Red Army after the May 3 mobilization. Between mid-May and mid-June, the Hungarian troops even conducted a victorious offensive in the north: at Salgótarján, Miskolc, Kassa, even as far as the Polish border. Clemenceau's two notes, of June 7 and June 13, respectively, succeeded in pressuring the Budapest government to stop the operations and eventually order the retreat of the army from the north. This decision was questioned at the time by Kun's comrades and later by his detractors. In any case, a solution "à la Brest-Litovsk," one that would save the regime of the Soviets at the cost of territorial concessions, was not feasible for Kun even if it had been supplemented by political concessions. The documents leave no doubt about the French determination to lance the Hungarian abscess; as in other questions, Clemenceau's firmness prevailed over the hesitations of his partners in the Council of Four, even if they successfully resisted the idea of an official intervention. In any event, this turned out to be unnecessary.

A Soviet regime in the heart of Central Europe; a defeated enemy country and suspected, no matter what its regime, of having hostile intentions toward its neighbors; ally of Soviet Russia and its potential military support; internally weak and threatened from abroad—the Hungary of the Councils had no chance to escape its fate. Furthermore, certain ambitions of Soviet Hungary could not but heighten the hostility of the allies, and that of France in particular. In fact, under the protection of the Hungarian Red Army under the command of Colonel Stromfeld, a Soviet Republic of Slovakia had just been proclaimed on June 16 at Eperjes, headed by Antonin Janoušek. At the same time communist emissaries from Budapest prepared, under the leadership of Dr. Ernö Bettelheim, a communist armed uprising in Vienna, in agreement with the Austrian communists. As a printing press in Budapest was printing counterfeit Austro-Hungarian crowns as fast as it could, money flowed freely in order to organize the seizure of power. However, the attempt failed prematurely—not only because of massive arrests on June 14, but also because the Workers' Council of Vienna refused to support it.[31]

Numerous attempts to overthrow the regime from within added to the difficulties of the government: revolts of peasants, of railway workers, and of the river flotilla on the Danube, among others. At the same time, anti-Bolshevik resistance, led particularly by Count Gyula Andrássy, became organized at Szeged—previously at Arad. Admiral Miklós Horthy, future Regent of Hungary, assumed command of the national army, which was composed mainly of officers' detachments and which was ready to march on the capital. The military defeat on the Tisza front at the hands of the Rumanian army sealed the fate of the dictatorship of the proletariat. On August 1, 1919, the Republic of the Councils fell. Béla Kun informed Lenin about the collapse in a dramatic telegram, the text of which, long kept secret, was published in the HCP newspaper *Népszabadság* on March 20, 1969, the fiftieth anniversary of the accession of the soviets of Hungary. "This turn of events [the overthrow of the Republic of the Councils] was caused on the one hand by the disintegration of our army, and on the other hand by the attitude of the proletariat itself, which was opposed to the dictatorship [of the proletariat]. When this happened, the situation was such that any fight would have been in vain in order to maintain the certainly authentic, but listless, dictatorship." The leaders and the most conspicuous militants sought refuge in Austria. For a quarter of a century, the history of the HCP was little more than the activities of the émigrés, who soon concentrated in Moscow. In Hungary itself, it was the often courageous, but insignificant, activity of the clandestine cells, which a handful of militants residing in the country and Comintern emissaries kept going.

The Clandestine Years: 1919-1945

As the main target of the repression that followed the downfall of the soviets of Hungary, the Hungarian Communist party was practically annihilated between 1919 and 1924, a period marked by two years of governmental instability followed by a slow consolidation under the government of Count István Bethlen.

In Hungary, few communist militants were able to escape the repression, which was carried out simultaneously by the established authorities, the officers' detachments under the high command of Admiral Horthy, and the volunteer corps that did not recognize his authority. The latter were especially active in Transdanubia, and Horthy's troops concentrated their activity first on the south, and eventually on the whole country. The white terror of 1919-1920 claimed an unknown number of victims, just as the red terror had previously. In the former, between 1,000 and 5,000 were killed, and several tens of thousands were imprisoned, often barbarously tortured before being put to death or in prison. How many of them were communists? This is even more uncertain. Documents and works on the history of the HCP furnish fragmentary information, but no general evaluation. They either state facts concerning a village, a factory, a region, or else they mention the atrocities committed against a group of militants or well-known personalities, for example, Otto Korvin, Jenö László, or the Lenin boys, who were executed after summary proceedings. In addition, the terror also came down upon Jews irrespective of their political inclination.[32]

Owing to various international demonstrations of solidarity with the victims of the repression and above all after the International Federation of Unions boycotted Hungary in the second half of 1920, numerous internees were freed.

Many of them later emigrated to Russia, Germany, France, and the United States. Moreover, in 1921 ten former condemned people's commissars as well as 400 other prisoners were exchanged for Hungarian officers who had been detained in Russia as prisoners of war.[33]

It was from Vienna that the HCP, or what remained of it after the collapse, tried to reorganize and secretly establish itself in Hungary. In fact, of the HCP's former Central Committee, only Otto Korvin and János Hirossik remained in Hungary, and, after Korvin's arrest, Hirossik remained there alone. The other leaders—with the exception of Szamuely, who, refused entry at the border, committed suicide—eventually reached Austria. Although they were interned for a few months at the Karlstein castle, Kun and his comrades constituted themselves as a Provisional Central Committee. Until the Comintern suspended it in March 1922, this Provisional Committee in Vienna changed its composition five times, chiefly because of fighting among the factions. As early as August 1921, the Executive Committee of the Comintern tried to settle the dispute by criticizing the two so-called factions of Kun and of Landler, but in vain. Until the First Congress of the reorganized HCP in Vienna in 1925, the battle among the factions continued unabated.

Kun and Landler differed more over questions of tactics and organization than over basic problems. No faction questioned the fundamental program of the party, which consisted in fighting the Horthy regime for a new proletarian revolution and a second dictatorship of the proletariat. What they argued about was how to attain these ends. "Kun's faction," one reads in the *History of the Revolutionary Workers' Movement*, "underestimated the activity of the communist groups in the country and insisted on the urgent formation of a clandestine [communist] mass party."[34] Its tactic, in response to this demand, was to send communist émigrés back to Hungary as well as former prisoners of war who had become communists in Soviet Russia. Landler's faction opposed this for the simple reason that the police easily apprehended the militants who went back, but also because they considered it premature to undertake an action of such magnitude directly after the failure of the 1919 dictatorship. They preferred the tactic of infiltrating the unions and even the Social Democratic party. The Comintern, itself divided, gave vague instructions trying to reconcile the two concepts, which were indeed incompatible. However, the resolution of August 1921 tilted the scale more toward Landler than toward Kun. Accent was placed on the necessity to come out of hiding on each occasion that presented itself and to utilize as much as possible legal means for the propagation of communist ideas.

Consequently, both tactics remained in force: the infiltration of the unions continued, and the policy of sending back militants clandestinely continued. Several agencies were created to direct the underground action in Hungary. These committees, or internal secretariats, were reorganized as often as the Central Committee itself, particularly because of the arrest of their members. Still, the fact remains that the committee directed by Ernö Gerö was able as early as 1922 to publish, at more or less regular intervals, clandestine communist papers such as the *Kommün* [Commune] as well as Young Communist papers such as *Ifju Proletár* [Young proletarian]. One committee, headed by Károly Öry, Kató Hámán, and Ignác Gögös, continued its activities even after the dissolution of the Central Committee in Vienna in 1922. After the Hungarian historian Agnes Szabó published an article in the bulletin for party history about "The First Congress of the Party of the Communists of Hungary" and its antecedents,[35] one of the party's former militants, Nandor Szekér, contested the official version about the composition of this committee of three members. According to his communication, which was also published in the bulletin, the "troika" was at first constituted in Hungary by Ignác Gögös, Kató Hámán, and Aladár Weiszhaus (whose name disappeared from the official version probably because of his "factionist" attitude) independent of the Vienna committee.[36] In 1923, on the other hand, Szekér went from Vienna to Budapest under the alias of "Heriszt," at the same time as Károly Öry. Only then did a genuine internal committee constitute itself: the two of them and Ignác Gögös as the third member.

But the central direction of the HCP—to the extent that one can speak of direction—shifted little by little from Vienna to Moscow. Most of the leaders and even simple militants reassembled in Moscow, where they again met their comrades released from the prisons of Hungary and exchanged against Hungarian officers detained as hostages by the Soviet government. From Moscow also came the initiative to form an Organization Bureau, at least until a party congress (then in preparation) elected a new Central Committee. According to Szabó's article, five persons belonged to the Organization Bureau in 1924: Gyula Alpári, János Hirossik, Béla Kun, Jenö Landler, and Mátyás Rákosi. Two of them, Hirossik and Landler, were then the leaders of the Vienna group of communist émigrés, Alpári was director of the *Inprekorr* (International Press Correspondence, a semiofficial Comintern agency) in Berlin, Rákosi one of the secretaries of the Executive Committee of the Comintern in Moscow, while Kun, member of the Executive Committee, had not participated at all in the direction of the Hungarian CP between 1922 and 1924. Consequently, the creation of the Organization Bureau marked a turning point in the history of the HCP.

The First Congress of the HCP took place in Vienna on August 18-21, 1925. The twenty-two delegates included five members of the Organization Bureau, fourteen delegates from the clandestine organizations in Hungary, and three from the organization in Vienna. The reports were presented by Gyula Alpári, Béla Kun, Jenö Landler, and Károly Öry. The congress decided on a platform, the major points of

which included the demand for a "worker-peasant" government and land reform while retaining the basic objective, that
is, the dictatorship of the proletariat. In addition to the more
well known leaders, three members of the Internal Secretariat
as well as Mátyás Rákosi and István Vági were elected members of the new Central Committee.

Vági was intimately linked to the existence and activity
of a crypto-communist party, the MSzMP, Magyar Szocialista
Munkáspárt (Hungarian Socialist Workers' Party), founded
shortly before the congress, in April 1925. With the help of
the public and legal activity of the MSzMP, the HCP undoubtedly extended its national and international audience.
The MSzMP did not have much success, it is true; but it tried
to get permission to present candidates for elections, it sent
its delegates to the congress of the Second International in
Marseilles, it attempted several times to establish a common
plan of action with the Social Democratic party, and it published periodicals, participated in the organization of social
struggles, and conducted an energetic agitation in the poorest
regions, particularly in the countryside. However, neither the
social democrats whom it solicited nor the authorities could
overlook the fact that it was communist. It had a history of
arrests and trials, which eventually paralyzed it as early as
1927.

Trials also mark the history of the HCP. The most spectacular, that of Mátyás Rákosi and his codefendants, was at
the same time the trial of the MSzMP because its leaders, including István Vági, were associated with it. The court
handed down twenty-nine convictions. Less than a year later,
in February 1927, police arrested seventy-two communists,
including Vági, who had just been released from prison, and
Zoltán Szántó, a member of the Internal Secretariat of the
HCP.

The leadership of the party was hardly more stable than
it had been before the First Congress. Between 1925 and
1930, date of the Second Congress, the composition of the

Central Committee changed as often as it had before. Georg Lukács, who had already belonged to the Provisional Committee, created after the collapse of the Republic of the Councils, was again delegated to it, as was one of his young followers, József Révai. The members of the Internal Secretariat succeeded each other in office because of the arrests. The organ that defined the actual political program of the HCP, namely, the Committee Abroad, which officially had its headquarters in Vienna, was still divided between the influence of its two most important members: Jenö Landler and Béla Kun. The latter, while commuting between Vienna and Moscow, was established in Moscow and drew his influence from his position on the Executive Committee of the Comintern.

In fact, the party hardly existed. In 1930, at the time of the Second Congress, it had about one thousand members, according to official estimates, which are in any case not reliable. Its direction was officially in Vienna: the Committee Abroad (which was at the same time "the nucleus of the Central Committee"). It was composed of a dozen persons, including Alpári, József Csapó, Ágoston Krejcsi, Kun, Lukács, Ernö Müller, Nándor Orosz, József Révai, and Imre Sallai. The party committee within Hungary worked under the direction of a secretary delegated by the Committee Abroad. During the years 1928-1932, Nándor Orosz, Mihály Háy, and Sándor Szerényi successively held the position of internal party secretary. After the Second Congress, this post became more important because the Internal Committee was no longer dependent on the Committee Abroad.[37]

At any rate, its limited membership and organizational inadequacies prevented the HCP from operating in a truly autonomous way. Thus its activity was reduced to propaganda efforts in a few unions, in the Social Democratic party, in various publications, and finally in such affiliated organizations as the Young Communists or such front organizations as the MSzMP. If the former remained relatively active even in the difficult period of the 1920s, the front organizations were a mere trifle after the disappearance of the MSzMP.

It was under these conditions that Georg Lukács submitted his proposals to the HCP; these are known as the "Blum Theses." Drafted after the Sixth Congress of the Comintern and the First Plenary Session of the Central Committee of the Hungarian CP in July 1928, the Blum Theses advocated a radical change in the party program. The central theme of our struggle, it maintained, must be "the democratic dictatorship of the proletariat and of the peasantry." To fight for a "democratic dictatorship" instead of declaring as immediate objectives the proletarian revolution and dictatorship—if these theses had been adopted, it would undoubtedly have changed the history of the HCP. But the Blum Theses were not adopted. An "Open Letter" of the Executive Committee of the Comintern addressed in the fall of 1929 to the members of the Hungarian CP gave its approval to the sectarian line of conduct that had prevailed in the Central Committee of the party. The "Open Letter" had moreover been written by Béla Kun, József Révai, and Sándor Szerényi, new secretary general of the party since that same year 1929.[38]

A few months later, from February 25 to March 15, 1930, the Second Congress of the HCP met at Aprelevka near Moscow. There were twenty delegates, some of whom had come from Hungary. The reports on the various party activities were presented by Béla Kun, Sándor Szerényi, József Révai, Márton Lovas, Ernö Normai, Hugó Kiss, Janka Bruck, as well as by comrade Fried, the representative of the Comintern. The numerous reports and long debates did not furnish much that was new. The HCP stayed with its traditionally sectarian and utopian line, which had no relation with the realities and the forces in Hungarian society.

The congress elected a Central Committee of fifteen members and five candidate members. But once again the list differs from one source to the other. We have recovered the following names: József Bergmann, Ferenc Boér, Zoltán Fürst, Miklós Juranovszky, Hugó Kiss, Béla Kun, Márton Lovas, Pál Nagy, Ernö Normai, József Pothornyik, József Oancz, István Rostás, Pál Sebes, Sándor Szerényi, and Antal Tisza.

Although it was elected by a regular congress, the new Central Committee was at once altered by the Comintern. In 1931, a Central Committee of eleven members took over the direction. Apart from Béla Kun and Pál Sebes, *none* of the Central Committee members elected by the Second Congress were in it. The newcomers were Sándor Fürst, Géza Gold, Ferenc Huszti, Frigyes Karikás, György Kilián, Károly Kiss, Sándor Poll, Imre Sallai, and József Tóth.[39]

In Hungary, as everywhere, the worldwide crisis of 1930-1933 created favorable ground for social and political agitation. The HCP undoubtedly knew how to profit from the situation, especially among the growing army of unemployed and among the agricultural workers, who were organized in an association with 2,000 members in 1930 and 4,000 in 1932. In addition to strikes and local demonstrations, which were often organized by the communists, the HCP played an important role in the great demonstration of September 1, 1930. In spite of the explosive social climate, no true unity of action could be achieved between the HCP and the Social Democratic party. The latter always wanted to keep its distance from the HCP in order to ensure its legal existence and to protect its power to act, particularly its press and its parliamentary representation. In 1921, a pact was concluded for that end between the prime minister, Count István Bethlen, on the one hand, and the SD party chief, Károly Peyer, on the other hand. The Social Democratic party later denounced this pact, but it nevertheless renewed under another form its agreements with the government. Above all, it always refused to conclude any alliance with the HCP. The communists for their part, while inviting the social democrats to cooperate, did not cease their violent attacks against the party and its

leaders, denouncing them in particular as "social-fascists."
The formation of a united organ of the opposition, the ESzE,
Egyesült Szakszervezeti Ellenzék [United Union Opposi-
tion], did not improve relations between the two parties
either. Finally; there was no common ground between their
respective forces. With its fourteen deputies, the SDP remained a fairly important parliamentary party, and it kept its
command over the unions, whose membership, very low in
1930 (87,000 as opposed to 200,000 in 1922), started to
climb again in the years of crisis.

In 1931, when martial law was proclaimed, the HCP's
clandestine activities began to encounter new and serious difficulties. In the summer of 1932, the police rounded up
members of the Internal Secretariat and other communists.
Their trial provoked vigorous international protests, which
were signed, among others, by Léon Blum, Romain Rolland,
H. G. Wells, Bertrand Russell, and Upton Sinclair. Two of the
defendants, Imre Sallai and Sándor Fürst, nevertheless received the death sentence and were executed on July 29,
1932.

Through its publications, the HCP achieved a modicum of
success in intellectual circles. The periodical *Uj Március* [New
March] (Vienna, 1925-1933), the review *Társadalmi Szemle*
[Social review] (1931-1933), the so-called central paper
Kommunista [Communist] (1928-1935), and the Young
Communist weekly *Ifju Proletár* had a substantial audience.
A literary review entitled *100%* (1927-1930) and the review
Gondolat [Thought] (1935-1937) attest to the HCP's cul-
tural activities, which were, however, limited by its sectarian
and dogmatic policies. For instance, the greatest communist
and national poet of the period, Attila József, was expelled
from the party in 1933.

In the second half of the 1930s, the stumbling block to
united action with the Social Democratic party remained, on
one hand, the problem of union opposition and, on the
other, the refusal of the SD leaders to deal with the commu-

nists. On the other hand, the HCP moderated its criticism and showed a certain flexibility in its attitude toward the SDP, to the same extent as the policy of the popular front was substituted for the policy of the "struggle between classes" within the international workers' movement. In January 1936, therefore, the HCP abandoned its opposition to the unions. However, the resolutions of the Seventh Congress of the Comintern of 1935, in adopting the program of the large antifascist popular fronts, provoked more confusion within the HCP than true progress toward unity.

In fact, starting with the arrest of the party's leaders and the execution of Sallai and Fürst in 1932, the HCP was in a state of permanent crisis. The delegates whom Moscow sent to take over (e.g., Sándor Poll) were also arrested. With the help of a new reorganization worked out in January 1933, new cadres, less known by the police, took matters under their responsibility but without constituting themselves as the Internal Secretariat. At the end of 1933, the HCP still had its Committee Abroad, which was in Berlin under the direction of Ferenc Huszti; its Central Committee, located for all practical purposes in Moscow and of which one member was delegated to direct the clandestine work in Hungary; its Budapest Committee; and its district committees, which directed the cells. In 1935, new arrests decimated the party, which induced the Comintern to take energetic measures, especially since the Hungarian communists had shown very little enthusiasm for the new "frontist" line. In May 1936, the Comintern dismissed the entire Central Committee of the Hungarian CP, which was guilty of having delayed the application of the Popular Front policy; it again entrusted a Provisional Secretariat headed by Zoltán Szántó with the reorganization of the party. The Comintern resolution also condemned the sectarian, bureaucratic, and antidemocratic methods of the party and the infighting that had raged among its leaders. In addition, the dismissed leaders had to account for their activities before the International

Control Commission of the Comintern. Béla Kun was particularly maltreated: the Comintern went so far as to prohibit his reelection to future leading organs.

This affair has still not been completely brought to light. According to a work on the evolution of the organization of the HCP (*Legyözhetetlen erö*), there were several contradictory resolutions in this respect. In its sessions of May 7-8, 1936, the Executive Committee of the Comintern is said to have delivered a less harsh judgment than the one by the Comintern's Secretariat, which met to treat Hungarian affairs first on June 23, then on June 26. Contrary to the Executive Committee, the Secretariat did not consider convening a conference of the Hungarian CP to elect a new central committee.[40]

For equally obscure reasons, the decision of the Comintern was transmitted to the leaders in Hungary as if the *party* itself had been dissolved, not just its Central Committee. Certain communist historians, e.g., Dezsö Orosz and István Pintér, dispute this version and maintain that the new HCP committee, which was established in Prague, had decided to dissolve the party; that the Comintern did not make the decision. In support of their interpretation, they quote a report addressed to the Comintern by Zoltán Szántó, secretary of the Prague committee. The report asserted particularly that because of circumstances "it was necessary to dissolve the entire party apparatus." It should be noted, however, that this report is dated February 1938, one year after the actual dissolution of the party; it by no means proves what organ had taken the decision. Zoltán Szántó, principal leader of the HCP at the time, in any case never admitted to having acted on his own. János Kádár, who was then only a young militant without title or rank, states—with regard to the second dissolution of the HCP in 1943—that in 1936 the dissolution had been carried out in a rather extraordinary way. "Secretly eight members of the party were retained" in order to prepare the reorganization. Since no one knew that despite the dissolution a small core of the HCP was thus preserved, the party lived "in a double clandestineness" toward both the authorities and its own former followers. But Kádár does not say who was behind this whole matter, the Executive Committee of the Comintern or the HCP committee in Prague.

Whichever it was, after the serious vicissitudes that had marked the entire history of the HCP since 1919, the decision of 1936 was the beginning of a complete disorganization, which practically was to last until the end of the war.[41]

The dissolution decree put an end to the activities of the Budapest Committee, the district and precinct committees, the communist cells, and the Young Communists. In the capital alone, 400 militants dependent upon the former Budapest Committee lost all contact with the party. The party press was likewise suppressed as well as the Committee Abroad residing in Berlin.

The work on the evolution of the party organization, (*Legyözhetetlen erö*), which for the first time disclosed this information to the public at large, admits the legitimacy of the reproaches the Comintern addressed to the HCP, but not the dissolution of the party. The decisions of the Comintern, according to this work authorized by the present Central Committee of the HCP, "are born in the period of [Stalinist] illegalities and of entirely fabricated trials." When they were taken, it continues, the resolutions of the Seventh Congress of the Comintern had in fact begun to be applied. It concludes that the consequences of the decision "impressed their unfortunate effects on the Hungarian communist movement until the beginning of the 1940s."[42]

The only remaining party organ—the Provisional Secretariat, composed of the secretary, Zoltán Szántó, and of two, later four, other members—established itself in Prague in July 1936. It remained there until shortly after the Munich agreements. Some members, such as József Révai, stayed there even until the German occupation. Its policy consisted in intensifying the activity of the communists in the legal workers' organizations, and chiefly in the Social Democratic party. At the same time, the party was becoming more and more oriented toward the leftist circles of the intelligentsia, and its relations with a democratic movement of populist persuasion, the Marciusi Front [March Front], were growing stronger. The review *Gondolat,* which represented the same "frontist" intellectual spirit, was forbidden by the government in November 1937. The organ of the Secretariat, the *Dolgozok Lapja* [Workers' journal], printed in Prague, appeared for a year between 1937 and 1938. With regard to the members of the Prague Secretariat—which was acting as Central Committee—Zoltán Szántó returned to Moscow, his successor Lajos Papp went to Paris in the spring of 1939, and István Friss and József Révai, after some intermediate stops, made their way to Moscow.

In the meantime, Ferenc Rózsa undertook the reorganization of the party in Hungary. He had the help of a delegate from the Prague Secretariat, Ferenc Házi, as well as that of other militants within the country—Gyula Kulich, Ferenc Donáth, József Turai, György Vértes, Gyula Tóth, Endre Sebestyén, István Kenéz, and others. Accessible documents and works do not reveal a great deal about the activity of the actual party secretary, Lajos Papp, who was in Paris. Sometime in 1939, however, the instructions came from Paris, and several militants, among others Ferenc Donáth and even Ferenc Rózsa himself, who was responsible for internal organization, went to the French capital in order to talk with the members of the Secretariat/Central Committee and its secretary Lajos Papp. In accord with the decisions taken in Paris, after three years of vacancy, a new directing organ was set up in Hungary under the name of "organ of political direction." It was headed by Ferenc Rózsa, and he was assisted by László Gács and István Kenéz. As for József Turai, he pursued his activities independently among the metalworkers. In the meantime, the Comintern, by a decision taken on June 10, 1939, and confirmed in January 1940,

ordered the HCP to reestablish its organizations under a central leadership. These resolutions did not, however, reach
Hungary—they were to be carried out in 1942 by Zoltán
Schönherz and his comrades from the Czechoslovak CP—and
so the HCP pursued its activities amid the confusion created
by the dissolution of 1936. Furthermore, the outbreak of the
war also put an end to the relations between communists in
Hungary and the members of the Prague Committee who had
succeeded in reaching Paris. In his memoirs, the secretary of
this committee, Lajos Papp, confirms that his relations with
the Hungarian CP came to an end in the winter of 1939, just
as with Moscow.[43] From this time on, until the end of the
war and his return to Hungary, he was active in the French
communist movement.

In order to reestablish a central leadership—and then for
a short time only—the HCP had to wait for the Comintern to
form a new secretariat, which was composed, as already mentioned, of Zoltán Schönherz, József Skolnik, and Sándor
Szekeres. In January 1941, these three communists formed
the new Central Committee. Skolnik acted as secretary
between January 1941 and December 1942; others who held
this position (until their respective arrests) were, in addition
to the members of the Secretariat, Ferenc Rózsa and László
Gács, and then, after Szekeres's suspension, Mihály Tóth.

This reorganization, attempted first from Paris and later
from Moscow, was all the more necessary since, through
Hitler's two arbitrations in Vienna and the annexation of sub-
Carpathian Ukraine, important Czechoslovak and Rumanian
territories were reunited with Hungary. This offered the HCP
new possibilities for action. The Czechoslovak regions alone
furnished a thousand militants, more than were in the
Hungarian CP itself. The less numerous communists of
northern Transylvania and those of the Yugoslav territories
occupied in 1941 were finally all incorporated, for some time
at least, in the HCP. Moreover, the party secretary, Skolnik,
and Schönherz came from the Czechoslovak party.

Apart from isolated cases, two great waves of arrests hit the HCP during this period. In April 1940, several hundred communists and, two years later, about 500-700 more were arrested and imprisoned. In June 1942, Rózsa fell into the hands of the police; in July, it was Schönherz's turn. The first was tortured to death, the second executed.

Among those who replaced them in the summer of 1942 were, as new members of the Central Committee, János Kádár, István Kovács, and István Szirmai. After the arrest of József Skolnik, Kádár was named party secretary. He was to hold this post until the next dissolution of the HCP.

For the HCP was again dissolved, for at least the fourth time in its history. On this occasion, it was by its own decision; it believed that after the dissolution of the Comintern in May 1943, it no longer had a raison d'être, at least under its present name and in its present form. In July 1943, a new party was born, the Peace party [Békepárt], which was headed by a Central Committee that included János Kádár, Gábor Péter, István Szirmai, Pál Tonhauser, Ferenc Donáth, and László Orbán. In September 1944, the HCP was reconstituted under its former name. László Rajk, Márton Horváth, Antal Apró, and Károly Kiss belonged to its Central Committee.

We shall not go into the controversies that took place within the HCP and its papers about the dissolution of the party in 1943, the activities of its successor, the Peace party, and finally the reconstitution of the HCP under its own name. After the war, the communists who returned from Moscow did not fail to reproach the leaders in Hungary for the party dissolution; according to them, the local leaders had misinterpreted the reason why the Soviet comrades had sacrificed the Comintern to the interests of the antifascist struggle. János Kádár soon paid the bill: the long years in prison that Rákosi and his comrades imposed on him. After his release and rehabilitation, he issued a restatement, which, as we have already pointed out, was published in the bulletin

for party history.[44] In it Kádár affirmed particularly that
after the great wave of arrests that struck the HCP in the
summer of 1942—we shall come back to this—only 10-12
communists of the 400-450 party members kept contact
among one another. This number rose afterward with great
difficulty to some seventy or eighty, but the arrest of the
secretary of the HCP's Budapest organization, István Kovács,
was again a severe setback. Although Kádár does not say it,
the Kovács affair meant the annihilation of what still remained of the party. Kádár calls attention to another point
of capital importance: since 1941 all communication between the HCP and Moscow was again interrupted until the
arrival of the Red Army in Hungary in 1944.

Under these circumstances, the dissolution of the HCP
and its transformation into the Peace party appeared to
Kádár and his friends to be the only way their hard-hit party,
which had only a symbolic existence, could survive.

Besides the successive reorganizations, other factors contributed to the chronic weakness of the party: the Comintern's mistrust, which, moreover, lay behind the numerous
dissolutions; the visceral sectarianism, heritage of the 1919
dictatorship, which hindered it, even after the Comintern
turned toward the antifascist fronts, to present a coherent
program capable of gaining ground in the country; the purges
and the Moscow trials, which decimated the Hungarian communists living in the emigration, a particularly important factor to which we shall come back later; and finally, the
German-Soviet pact of 1939.

The documents and works published in Hungary after
1945 hardly mention the disappointment and confusion
caused by the reversal of Soviet politics in August 1939. Even
in the pamphlets destined for the various party training
schools in the course of the 1950s, that is, in the middle of
the Stalinist period, a certain discretion may be noted in this
respect. "By this treaty," according to one of these pamphlets, "the wise Stalinist policy for some time ensured peace

for the Soviet people. . . . After the conclusion of the agreement . . . the relations between the Soviet Union and the
Hungarian government improved somewhat. Our party
turned this to an advantage in order to make the Soviet
Union known and popularize it by legal means."[45] It took a
truly disingenuous author, in this case Gyula Kállai, to affirm
that "the Party of the Communists of Hungary considered
the German-Soviet nonaggression pact as an act of great importance not only from the point of view of the Soviet
Union, but also from that of Hungary." More discreet, but
also more accurate, the authors of the *History of the Hungarian Revolutionary Workers' Movement* admit, while
defending Soviet politics, that "in the beginning, an important part of the workers received with incomprehension the
unforeseen conclusion of the pact . . . ; the latter provoked
temporary confusion even among a part of the communists,
who only later understood the necessity and correctness of
this step."[46]

In fact, the pact permitted, among other things, the publication of Soviet books in Hungary. It gained the release of
Mátyás Rákosi and his transfer to Moscow in exchange for
the flags of the Hungarian War of Independence of 1848-
1849, which had been seized by the armies of Tsar Nicholas
I. They were returned in the spring of 1941.

Hungary's entry into the war against the Soviet Union on
the side of Germany made life more difficult for the HCP,
but clarified its situation. Henceforth the HCP's antifascist
propaganda and its attempts to organize a democratic front
for peace acquired a certain credibility, although little success. Among the actual results, one must note a certain communist influence on the social democratic left, and in particular the edition of the 1941 "frontist" Christmas number
of *Népszava* [The word of the people], the SDP daily,
published with the collaboration of numerous communist
intellectuals. Another success was the creation of the Hungarian Committee for Historical Commemoration, which, using

the occasion of the national holidays, especially March 15, 1942, organized patriotic demonstrations against the war and against Hungary's dependence on Hitlerian Germany. Among the noncommunists on the committee, one finds for the first time certain personalities who were to play a role in Hungary during the democratic coalition of 1945: for example, the future president of the Council of Ministers, Ferenc Nagy, the future president of the Republic, Árpád Szakasits, the great historian and future ambassador to Moscow, Gyula Szekfü, and others.

After the Germans occupied Hungary on March 19, 1944, the HCP, acting under the name of the Peace party, launched an appeal for resistance. In fact, until the advance of the Soviet army, there had been very little resistance in Hungary; at most there had been acts of sabotage. On the other hand, the party made some progress in the area of lining up antifascist forces and in the preparation of a democratic postwar period. The movement, initiated in 1942, gained momentum after the turning point of Stalingrad and even more in 1944, when, after the German occupation of the country, the opposition parties were dissolved. The communists, more accustomed to clandestine activities than the partisans of other parties, established contact with certain personalities of the opposition parties and with them eventually created the Hungarian Front.

In Moscow, under the direction of the Soviets, the survivors of the great purges of the 1930s also prepared for this postwar period.

The HCP's "Moscow history" has never been written. It would be necessary to collect all documents relating to the rehabilitation of the purge victims in order to reconstruct this history, although hundreds of cases of simple militants, without title or rank, would remain in the dark. The only work that examines all aspects of what life in Moscow was like for the Hungarian communists who had sought refuge in the Soviet Union is the first volume (withdrawn from circulation) of Endre Sik's autobiography. As the former minister of foreign affairs in the Kádár administration, Endre Sik is undoubtedly a genuine eyewitness of these years of darkness, but he, too, can have known only a limited number of cases, those of his personal acquaintances. But there were probably several thousand Hungarian communists in the Soviet Union. Only a small fraction of these émigrés worked in the apparatus of the Comintern, in its schools, its publishing firms, at the Marx-Engels Institute, and other well-known central institutions. In recent works these collaborators of the central organs have reappeared in short, stereotyped biographical notes: "in 193– he became a victim of the illegalities of the Stalinist period."[47]

The HCP in Power

Only a tiny proportion of the communist militants returned to Hungary in 1945; the Stalinist purges had decimated their ranks more than the police and the courts of the Horthy regime had. Some of them went back to Hungary by parachute. In fact, a handful of courageous militants came back to form guerrilla units behind the German lines. Among the many who perished were Richárd Rózsa and György Kilián. Others survived, such as Zoltán Fodor and Sándor Nógrádi. Another group of Hungarians came back in the ranks of the Soviet Army and its services: the writer Béla Illés, a colonel, and the editorial staff of *Uj Szó* [New word], the Hungarian paper of the Soviet Army. The political leaders returned in several waves, the first of which included Ernö Gerö, József Révai, Mihály Farkas, and Imre Nagy. Mátyás Rákosi himself came back only in 1945, followed by others.

By whom and how was this general staff formed? After he returned to the USSR from the prisons of Horthy, Rákosi was recognized as leader of the Hungarian faction of Moscow, and he kept his important post with the personal assent of Stalin, perhaps even under his command. But Ernö Gerö, an old hand of the Comintern and probably of the secret service, also had solid connections. According to certain rumors, he had as much power as Mátyas Rákosi, the top-ranking official, if not more. Mihály Farkas was probably promoted by the influential circles of the Komsomol, and Imre Nagy, it appears, had free access to Molotov. Apart from the struggles for influence, which organ or what person chose this staff and solved the delicate question of hierarchy? The documents we have do not tell us.

In any case, the four from Moscow who arrived first set themselves up as Provisional Central Committee as early as November 5, 1944, in Szeged. They moved to Debrecen in December and remained there until March 1945. In the meantime, on January 19, another Central Committee had been formed in Budapest by Antal Apró, Bertalan Barta, Márton Horváth, János Kádár, Gyula Kállai, Károly Kiss, István Kossa, István Kovács, Gábor Péter, and Zoltán Vas. With the exception of Vas, they all were militants from within Hungary who were coming out of hiding. The secretary of the HCP, László Rajk, who had been arrested in December 1944, was still in prison. The two Central Committees united on February 23. Rákosi became the secretary of the new committee. We shall come back to these two parallel central committees in chapter 2.

The number of members belonging to the HCP after it emerged from the underground is uncertain: 3,000, according to a speech by Rákosi; a hundred or even less, according to others. The membership certainly increased with an incredible speed. At the end of 1945, the HCP already had 500,000 members. But its real strength lay elsewhere, in Soviet power, i.e., in the Red Army and in the international political authority of the Allied Control Commission presided over by Marshal Voroshilov. The HCP, however weak it was numerically, was the agent of this immense power. But it would be a serious error to underestimate other elements, namely, the force of the organization, propaganda, and operation of the HCP itself. It was the only political party that knew what it wanted, that had a program, an ideology, and a model of organization and operation. In the general confusion of the period, these could only be assets. The following chapters will treat this point and the HCP's political operation, which henceforth was intertwined with the history of the country itself. Here we treat only the major steps.

From 1945 to 1947, even to the beginning of 1948, the HCP, like the other communist parties of Central and Eastern Europe, followed a popular front policy and took part in a governmental coalition composed of four democratic parties. The HCP held three ministerial posts. In subsequent administrations, it had five, in addition to the chairmanship of the High Council for Economics. Its internal history was marked by the National Conference of May 20, 1945, and later by the Third Congress of the party, which was held from September 28 to October 1, 1946, under the banner of the struggle against the reaction—which meant fight against the troublesome elements of the other parties in the governmental coalition, including the Social Democratic party. From 1947, the unification of the two parties was on the agenda, despite opposition from most socialist leaders.

Incapable of resisting the HCP's pressure, the SDP eventually yielded. Its so-called rightist leaders resigned. On June 12, 1948, concurrently held congresses of the two parties agreed to the union. On the same day, they met in a united congress. The new party was formed, and until the events of 1956 it carried the name of Magyar Dolgozók Pártja, MDP [Hungarian Workers' party].

Until the unification of the two parties, the direction of the HCP had changed little from its composition in 1945, except that part of the 1945 Central Committee constituted itself in 1946 as a Politburo of nine members, while the others remained members of an enlarged Central Committee. In the Politburo, elected at the close of the Third Congress of the HCP, the Moscow group held five positions out of nine; it also dominated the General Secretariat as well as the Committee for Organization charged with directing the apparatus. In fact, it was not the entire Moscow team, but the quadrumvirate of Rákosi-Gerö-Révai-Faraks, that controlled the party —with the help of a dedicated and strictly led apparatus.

In the unified party, a few former so-called leftist social democrats held a certain number of high posts, but the principles of organization and the true power hierarchy remained unchanged.

Practically alone in the possession of power, the HCP shifted toward openly Stalinist policies from the beginning of 1948. Nationalizations, projects for forced industrialization, the beginnings of agricultural collectivization, massive purges and arrests, the *gleichschaltung* of the intellectuals—we see the same characteristics in Hungary as in the other people's democracies. Hungary, too, became a people's democracy. The political turn went hand in hand with an ideological reinterpretation of the new society and the new state. The question no longer was, as before, to construct a "new democracy," but rather to construct a "people's democracy," erecting socialism with the help of the dictatorship of the proletariat and its vanguard, the Communist party. One year later, in 1949, when nearly all the former leftist socialist leaders who had adhered to the unified party had already rejoined the former leaders of the democratic parties in the prisons or in the tombs, those communists who were judged dangerous or cumbersome began to be eliminated. The Rajk trial of October 1949 opened a long period of liquidations within the HCP itself.

After Stalin's death, the Hungarian CP again went through a period that, in more than one respect, distinguished it from the other communist parties. In June 1953, the HCP leaders were summoned to Moscow in the company of one of their disgraced comrades, Imre Nagy. The Hungarian delegation was received in the Kremlin by the complete

Soviet Party Presidium: Beria, Khrushchev, Malenkov, Mikoyan, Molotov. This was the collapse of the whole system that Rákosi and his companions had constructed. The Soviet comrades heaped criticism on those who were most responsible for Stalinist policies and compelled them to "correct their mistakes" in every respect and to share power with Imre Nagy. Rákosi kept his post of secretary general of the party, but Nagy took his place at the head of the government.

Thus the era of reforms began. It was marked by the amelioration of the economic and political situation in the country, by the release of thousands of political prisoners, and by the relentless fight between the Stalinist faction and the liberal faction led by Imre Nagy. Eighteen months later, in the spring of 1955, Imre Nagy was relieved of his duties, sweeping away with his fall the politics of reform as well as a great number of his collaborators. This neo-Stalinist interlude was not to last. After the Twentieth Congress of the Soviet CP, the liberal wing of the party slowly regained the ascendancy at the same time that unrest was increasing among the population. The October events in Poland were the catalyst. On October 23, 1956, Budapest experienced the greatest mass demonstration in its history. During the night, arms reigned supreme. The battle raged for six days. In the meantime, Gerö, who had replaced Rákosi in the preceding June, in turn yielded his post to János Kádár. Imre Nagy, all of a sudden reinstated in the Politburo of the party, was again appointed president of the Council of Ministers. During a truce of barely six days, Imre Nagy reestablished the former governmental coalition with the democratic parties, won over the insurgents to his program, restored order, and negotiated the retreat of the Soviet troops. But after these few days of precarious independence, the Soviet tanks again moved out to attack the capital. The desperate resistance of a few thousand insurgents and of some units of the Hungarian army could not stop them. The Soviet intervention of November 4 marked the end of the revolution.

The HCP, as an organization, vanished in the first hours of combat on the night of October 23. Of its powerful apparatus, only a few officials remained, barricaded behind the doors of the Central Committee headquarters, which was guarded by Soviet tanks. It was the same in the provinces. Once more, the HCP was dissolved, and from its ashes a new communist party was formed: the Magyar Szocialista Munkáspárt [Hungarian Socialist Workers' party], a name it still retains today. "The new party," János Kádár, secretary general, proclaimed on November 2 over the radio, "breaks with the crimes of the past." A directing committee undertook the organization of the MSzMP and prepared a general congress for the founding of the party. It was composed of Ferenc Donáth, János Kádár, Sándor Kopácsi, Géza Losonczy, Georg Lukács, Imre Nagy, and Zoltán Szántó. Two of them, Kádár and Szántó, had been secretaries of the HCP at different periods in its history; three, namely, Lukács, Nagy, and Szántó, had returned from Moscow in 1945. Lukács and Szántó belonged to the founding fathers of the Republic of the Councils in 1919. Nagy had been a member of the Politburo of the party in 1945 and again in 1953. Six out of the seven had at different times been members of the Central Committee. Instead of *Szabad Nép* [Free people], the party launched a new daily newspaper, the *Népszabadság* [People's freedom].

On the night of November 2, János Kádár broke with his comrades, went to the Soviet Union, and a few days later came back to Hungary at the head of a new government, which soon established itself in Budapest. But he did not dissolve the MSzMP. In a rather paradoxical situation, *Népszabadság* appealed to the members of the MDP (the name of the HCP before the revolution) to reorganize the party. At once a new Provisional Central Committee was created, and the members of the old one, with the exception of Kádár, were first sent to supervised exile in Rumania, then to the prisons of Hungary, where Imre Nagy was executed. Géza

Losonczy died in prison.

The new MSzMP, "János Kádár's party," was thus established in Hungary shortly after the Soviet intervention of
November 4, 1956. It would have great difficulties in imposing itself as the sole governing party, as the depository of
socialism and the national destiny. In 1956, before the
October events, the party had about 800,000 members, that
is, nearly as many as in the preceding five years. On December 1, the party registers listed 37,818 adherents, that is,
less than 5 percent of the previous membership. According to
official estimates, the actual number was slightly higher,
namely, about 50,000-60,000, which would be 7 percent.[48]
Whatever it was, the loss was severe, even if, owing to a recovery, the number of registered communists was to rise
rapidly later on and reach 125,000 in mid-January 1957,
345,000 in June, more than 400,000 the following year, and
more than 500,000 in 1966.

The initial decrease in the number of adherents was a
consequence of yet other difficulties. The party had lost its
credit and its authority not only with the great majority of
the population, but also among its former members. Besides,
Kádár and his team inspired little confidence among the
former Stalinists and even less among the partisans of Imre
Nagy, who felt betrayed. In addition, the mistrust was recip-
rocal: the MSzMP by no means solicited the participation of
the "rightists" and at the same time kept a certain distance
toward the left wing of the former party. A few former
Stalinists, high officials of the regime during the era of
Rákosi and Gerö, were barred from access to the party, and
some were even dismissed, especially in the ranks of the political police. However, the main body of the apparatus resumed its place with, here and there, some new departmental
heads.[49]

More important changes occurred at the top of the party
at the National Conference of June 27-29, 1957, the Seventh
Congress of November 30-December 5, 1959, the Eighth

Congress of November 20-25, 1962, the Ninth Congress of November 28–December 3, 1966, and the Tenth Congress of 1970.

These changes will later be examined from the point of view of organization and social composition. For the moment the principal political fact must be noted: stability at the top. Until the Tenth Congress of 1970, the Politburo majority were men "of the first hour," members of the Executive Committee of November 1956, members of the Central Committee reelected by the Conference of 1957 and the Seventh Congress of 1959: Antal Apró, Béla Biszku, Lajos Fehér, Jenö Fock, János Kádár, Gyula Kállai as well as György Aczél, L. Czinege, Sándor Gáspár, Pál Ilku, Zoltán Komócsin, Dezsö Nemes, Károly Németh, Rezsö Nyers, and István Szirmai, members or candidate members of the first central committees of 1957 and 1959. At least ten other persons also appeared again for ten years in key party positions: the economists István Friss and Miklós Ajtai, the high party officials László Orbán and Arpád Pullai, the ministers Endre Sik, Géza Révész, and others. As for Ferenc Münnich, cofounder with Kádár of the "revolutionary workers' and peasants' government," he retired, like Miklós Somogyi, in consideration of his age, but also because of his differences with Kádár.

There was stability at the top and, let us add, at the center. Those with whom Kádár and his closest collaborators were forced to part with along the way found themselves at one time or another implicated in so-called factionist conspiracies against the middle line of Kádár. One of the first, Imre Dögei, minister of agriculture of the Kádár administration of November 1956, was excluded from the Central Committee in May 1960 and from the party two years later. There were other conspiracies as well. It has come to light that Mátyás Rákosi, after being exiled to the Soviet Union, attempted to resume relations, either personally or through intermediaries, with his former followers in order to incite them to oppose Kádár and his collaborators. Another spectacular case is that of György Marosán, former leftist social democrat who had joined the HCP in 1948, who was imprisoned by Rákosi, released and rehabilitated by Nagy, and promoted to member of the Politburo by Kádár. Marosán himself fell in 1962 under circumstances that are still unclear. In any case, his fall coincided with another campaign against Kádár, this time on a wider scale than the previous ones. Owing to the unconditional support of Khrushchev, Kádár triumphed once more, and the Eighth Congress of the HCP assembled in the fall of 1962 and confirmed his politics all along the line, especially "the energetic administrative measures" that had been taken against those who "by their factionist attempts had wanted to make the party deviate from the path of Marxist-Leninist politics." Indeed, the "Instructions of the Central Committee of the Hungarian Socialist Workers' Party for the Congress"[50] stressed the need to pursue the "struggle on two fronts," that is, against rightist revisionism and leftist sectarianism simultaneously. In reality, it was the left that was singled out, not only by concrete measures but also by certain declarations (see below).

Three other serious crises remain to be mentioned. The dismissal of Khrushchev in October 1964 did not fail to shake Kádár's position. Moreover, he was the only party boss of the people's democracies who took the liberty to criticize if not the substance, at least the form, of the decision that hit his powerful protector. But once again, he remained at the head of the party, the new Soviet leaders having fully understood the usefulness of keeping him in power. Four years later, when Dubček's Czechoslovakia was invaded by Warsaw Pact troops (among which were Hungarian units), Kádár again played a rather enigmatic role. He first tried to mediate: to bring Dubček back "to reason" while trying to curb the interventionist inclinations of his opponents. He later played a disapproving role, if only by his strange, temporary disappearance directly after the armed uprising of August 20,

1968. In addition to the painful feelings that the Hungarian intervention and participation inspired in him, Kádár had to fear the repercussions of the Czechoslovak affair on his own politics. Was it not the Hungarian CP that practiced, well before the Prague Spring, if not "a communism with a human face," at the very least a liberal politics with a certain respect for the personality of the citizen? Was it not the Hungarian CP that, almost at the same time as the Czechoslovaks, began an extensive economic reform, called the "new economic mechanism," that aimed at decentralization and profitability? Once more, Kádár surmounted the crisis and even seemed to emerge from it with increased authority, which permitted him to pursue his liberal politics unhindered: in the internal life of the party against the old dogmatics; in economics; in cultural life, where the Hungarians enjoyed liberties unknown to their socialist neighbors; as well as in political life. The only price the Hungarian CP had to pay for Moscow's toleration of its line was as before, namely, unconditional alignment with Soviet foreign policy. Liberal within, the Hungarian CP without hesitation supported Moscow's policies toward Peking, Bonn, Jerusalem, Bucharest, and other sensitive world capitals.

However, the Stalinist opposition was not disarmed by that. It only waited for a favorable moment to attack the leading circles and Kádár himself as far as it could reach him. An important part of the Central Committee elected by the Tenth Congress in 1970 even appeared to favor the theses of the "left" opposition, so much so that János Kádár made known his desire to resign, especially in 1972. Ruse or genuine discouragement? Whatever it was, in this year of internal crisis, Kádár dominated once more while launching a new challenge to his opponents. In a speech delivered on the occasion of his sixtieth birthday before a select audience, he returned to the basic analysis of the events of 1956 that he had made fifteen years before, laying stress not only on the "counterrevolutionary" character, but also on the "tragic" character of the great popular movement.[51]

A popular personality in spite of the role he played in November 1956, architect of a new liberal policy, skillful politician, Kádár has until now survived, but at the price, it appears, of numerous concessions. Since 1972, the HCP has had to curb the development of the "new economic mechanism" and restrict cultural liberties. A group of sociologists, headed by Rákosi's former prime minister, András Hegedüs, was dismissed; writers were reprimanded and, for the first time in almost fifteen years, arraigned in court. Many signs portended a hardening of the general politics of the HCP, a hardening that was further accentuated after the "ideological conference" of the communist parties held in Moscow in December 1973. In March 1974, in fact, Kádár had to agree, after a resolution of the Central Committee, to separate himself from several of his most intimate collaborators, including György Aczél, in charge of cultural affairs, and Rezsö Nyers, the real head of the new economic course. In a speech given on March 28, Kádár indeed stressed that "the principal direction of our politics remains unchanged and without break." However, the CC resolution's emphasis on the necessity to "strengthen the leading role of the working class" in all domains, including cultural life, may well indicate that the question was really a readjustment of the party "line" to the prejudice of intellectual liberties—and perhaps other liberties —which the citizens of Hungary still enjoy.

The Eleventh Party Congress, which met from March 17 to March 22, 1975, as well as the policy pursued since this date, has finally dissipated these fears. Still, a muffled opposition against the Kádár policy expressed itself during this congress, and it is improbable that some of the potential leaders of a harder line might have speculated on his fall. Kádár himself hinted at it in a short sentence of his closing speech. "There was a lot of criticism concerning economic problems," said Kádár, "and sometimes I believed that the opposition had taken the platform."[52] Kádár's general line was not attacked, but his way of dealing with particular problems was criticized—such as the shortcomings of the steel industry or the deficiencies in the food industry. The dismissal of Jenö Fock, president of the Council of Ministers, shortly after the congress was probably because the economic shortcomings reported by some of the delegates to the congress, but there were no other major consequences. Moreover, the "opposition" speakers never criticized either the person or the policy of János Kádár. Sándor Gáspár and Károly Németh, the leaders of this tendency, expressed themselves with great moderation during the congress. If there had ever been a "conspiracy," Kádár thwarted it once again, thanks to his political skill in avoiding conflicts, to the undeniable success of his politics, and, in the last run, thanks to the support the Soviet Union extended to him in spite of his deviations. Brezhnev himself attended the Eleventh Congress in order to pay tribute to the Hungarian leader.

Since then the position of Kádár seems as solid as a rock. With Kim Il-sung of Korea, Kádár is the oldest CP leader in power. He has held his position since 1956; Gierek, Husak, Honecker, and the others, including Brezhnev himself, are newcomers by comparison.

Owing to its economic achievements, Hungary has become, after East Germany, the most prosperous socialist country and has a more or less satisfied population. Its system of agriculture is unique in Eastern Europe: collective agriculture no longer encounters peasant opposition, and owing to the extraordinary flourishing of the Hungarian kolkhozes, there is enough food on the market. All this produces a relatively serene political climate, unlike that of all the other countries of the socialist bloc. If Kádár were disavowed or, even worse, removed from his functions, it would be tantamount to the disavowal of the *only* somewhat successful communist experiment. Neither the leftist opposition to Kádár within the party nor the leaders of the Kremlin would risk such a dangerous path. Kádár will, consequently, retain his post and can even feel free to differ in language and deviate in his political line, both of which make him a hero of a rather original form of communism. Natural factors, that is, his age and state of health, threaten this experiment, and not his eventual discredit. Who will succeed him? Nobody can answer this question. There seems to be no designated successor. Nevertheless, one thing seems certain: Kádár favors the young, the new elite of the party, instead of the "old revolutionary guard."

2. The Role and Organization of the Party

. **Status**

The strength of the HCP has never been its popularity among the voters. After it came to power in 1919, it organized, between April 7 and April 12, general elections with secret ballots and universal suffrage. Even at that time, however, single lists were used. Consequently, the official lists prevailed without difficulty. Thus Hungary elected its councils, or soviets, at all lower levels: villages, towns, precincts, and districts. The local councils then elected delegates to the councils of the counties and of the major cities, which in turn sent their delegates to the National Assembly of Councils, the "parliament" of the dictatorship of the proletariat. There is nothing astonishing in the fact that neither communist nor social democratic works insist much on the democratic character of the 1919 elections.[1] Afterward, for a quarter of a century, the minuscule, illegal HCP did not think for a moment of appealing to the voters—except to dissuade them from voting social democratic. The attempts of the crypto-communist party MSzMP to stand in elections failed.

In 1945, for the first and only time in its history, the HCP participated in free elections: municipal elections in October, general elections in November. In the first, communists and socialists presented single lists and carried off

43 percent of the vote in Budapest. In the second, held in the whole country and on separate lists, the communists got 17.4 percent of the votes, the social democrats nearly as many. The big winner, the Party of the Smallholders, won convincingly with more than 57 percent of the vote. Seventy communist deputies and 69 socialist deputies sat in parliament opposite 245 smallholder deputies and 2 liberals. The HCP could also count on the if not unconditional, at least relatively certain support of the 23 deputies of the National Peasant party. Let us further note that the other political parties, among which were the Szabadság párt [Freedom party] and the Keresztény demokrata néppárt [People's Christian Democratic party] supported by the Catholic church, did not participate in the elections. Under these conditions, the votes obtained by the Party of the Smallholders included the specific votes for the party—as a member of the governmental coalition—as well as those of the opposition, which could express itself only by voting neither communist nor socialist. In 1947, communist electoral tactics were to admit them to the elections precisely in order to divide the enormous bloc of the smallholders.

These facts have a certain importance: they are the only way to measure the electoral influence of the HCP in the new Hungary, one year after its emergence from the underground. They show an influence certainly not negligible, but extremely limited. The intense anticommunist propaganda of the Horthy regime and the excesses of the red terror of 1919 undoubtedly had something to do with it. On the other hand, the extreme moderation of the communists, the HCP's national and democratic, rather than revolutionary, program, its indisputable dynamism in the reconstruction of the country, the land reform, its level of organization, and lastly its skillful propaganda, could counterbalance the negative effects. All things considered, the result of the 1945 elections probably reflected the real relation of political forces: the HCP was at the head of the medium-sized parties, but it was far from having a truly national audience. It represented certain social categories and groups more than it did vast social classes, that is, it represented a part of the urban proletariat (but a smaller part than the SDP represented), the poor peasantry of certain traditionally radical regions, and finally an important part of the Jewish electorate. Of the 800,000 votes it obtained, less than a quarter came from Budapest, which illustrates at the same time the HCP's weakness in the only great workers' stronghold—the capital—and its relative popularity in the provinces.

The elections after 1945 do not allow us to draw any conclusion. Already in 1947, they were not entirely falsified, but they were distorted by the use of "blue" ballots, enabling a certain number of communist voters—carefully selected—to vote twice. In the end, the HCP benefited little by this, because the fraud only produced very few additional votes but in return deprived the HCP of an important part of the credit and the confidence that it had previously held. After this date, Hungary has had only fictitious elections having no relation whatsoever to public opinion.

What then is the HCP? It is impossible to define its "status" according to the norms and notions of Western political science. The last indications about its electoral bases date from thirty years ago. It is not a revolutionary party: on the one hand, it is the sole holder of power, and, on the other hand, its organization, its roots, and its operation are highly bureaucratic. From the sociocultural point of view, it is likewise impossible to define it with precision. Is it really a party of the proletariat, as ideological tradition has it? It has never been such in the past, and nothing indicates that its recent evolution has made it the authentic representative of a working class that is utterly different from the prewar proletariat. The HCP's constant concern to justify itself at least by means of a preponderance of workers among its followers continues to clash with this indifference—or with this dissatisfaction—even today, as its social composition shows. Does it exist, then, primarily for the sake of the party apparatus itself, does it attempt to conduct the state affairs as best it can as much as circumstances permit? For the time being, until we have more information with which to work, we shall have to be content with this summary definition.

At no time in its history has the HCP been tolerated. Even in the brief period between its formation in November 1918 and its accession to power in March 1919, it suffered from acts of intolerance, even repression; after all, its leader came to power directly from the prisons of Count Károlyi's democratic republic. The HCP has never had an alternative other than illegality or power. Its political aspirations certainly changed according to circumstances, as we shall see. But even when it supported antifascist tendencies, as between 1941 and 1944, or "advanced" democratic tendencies, as between 1945 and 1948, its fundamental aspiration remained the same: power, either undivided or partial.

Membership

At its lowest ebb, the HCP had at most several hundred adherents. This was true in the mid-1920s, when the repression had practically annihilated its organizations. It was true in 1936 when the Comintern dissolved the party. It was true, finally, after the successive losses of the 1940s, before the end of the war. The 3,000 members at the end of 1944 (given in the official history of the HCP) is a maximum estimate and cannot be relied upon. But even if this estimate were accurate, the HCP would no less remain an entirely insignificant party from the point of view of its membership while underground: 0.05 percent of the adult population.

At its highest level, before the influx of the social democrats, the party had 743, 836 members (August 1947). In the summer of 1948, just before unification, it had 887,472 members (the already emaciated SDP then numbered 240,658). Finally, the unified party (the MDP) had 1,128,130 members, that is, 12 percent of the entire population of Hungary. The HCP then undertook a vast review of its membership, which resulted in 179,000 exclusions, to which must be added some 130,000 who had failed to present themselves to the review commission. More than 100,000 of those admitted were at the same time qualified as candidates. In all, 756,588 persons were admitted as full members and 124,156 as candidates, consequently, a total of 880,744.[2] According to the same official sources, between the reviews of the summer of 1948 and the fall of 1950, the unified HCP recorded another decrease of about 70,000 members, due, besides the deaths, to new exclusions as well as to the fact that a certain number of admitted members and candidates (about 30,000) had not presented themselves to pick up their membership books.[3] After all these fluctuations, the membership has become stable at around 850,000-900,000 members and candidates. Table 1 is a summary and Table 2 shows the evolution of the membership after 1954, as established from various official sources.[4]

Table 1

	Jan. 1950	Jan. 1951	Jan. 1952	Jan. 1953	July 1953
Members	698,344	699,688	760,080	775,447	789,707
Candidates	130,351	162,426	185,526	130,640	95,490
Total	828,695	862,114	945,606	906,087	885,197

Table 2

	Jan. 1954	Jan. 1955	Jan. 1956	Jan. 1957	Jan. 1959	Jan. 1962
Members	808,223	811,135	820,004	101,806	385,430	467,459
Candidates	54,380	42,406	39,033		31,216	31,185
Total	862,603	853,541	859,037	101,806	416,646	498,644

	Nov. 1966	June 1970	Jan. 1975
Total	584,849	662,397	754,353

After the HCP almost disappeared during the revolution of 1956, its membership increased abruptly between 1957 and 1959. Thereafter, the rate of increase was slower.

As for the exclusions, which were rare before 1948, they became massive when the unified party was "purified" in 1949. According to *Legyözbetetlen erö,* of the 178,850 who were excluded, more than 50,000 were workers, 23,000 peasants, and almost 14,000 intellectuals. Some 90,000 in the miscellaneous category were excluded. Between 1948 and 1956, more than 350,000 members were excluded from the party, some 40,000 between 1954 and 1956. There have been relatively few exclusions in the new communist party MSzMP.

Since Hungary has about 10 and a half million inhabitants, it is easy to calculate the percentages: at the maximum 12 percent, on the average 6-8 percent, at the least 1 percent of the entire population belonged to the HCP in power, as opposed to 0.05 percent in the darkest underground years before the war.

In 1948, in order to overcome the inherent disadvantages of a mass party, the HCP introduced a special category of members, that of activists called "party workers." Their number reached 106,859 in 1948, 20 percent of whom were women, according to the registers; but according to another estimate, their actual number amounted to some 125,000. This corresponded roughly to the party apparatus with its paid officials plus a certain number of communist activists who worked for the state: army officers, company directors, presidents of cooperatives. The category of activist (provided with a special card) was eventually abolished. There remained the apparatus proper, comprising the officials of the Central Committee apparatus as well as of the committees of the towns, of the counties, of the districts, and of the large companies. At its zenith the MDP numbered some 20,000 organizations. It is impossible to draw conclusions from this concerning the number of paid officials. All the secretaries of cells are not "independent" officials, that is, paid by the party. In the small factory or neighborhood cells, the members of the bureau are in general workers who perform their function in the party organization as volunteers. Besides, the party requires its members to do a certain amount of "social work" voluntarily. The paid officials are destined for the more important organizations at the level of the precincts in cities, at the level of the municipal administration in the villages, and at the level of the ministries in the state apparatus. The greatest concentration of paid officials is found, except for the central apparatus, at the middle level, i.e., in the county committees and the large cities. The apparatus of the Budapest committee, for example, has always been a kind of second municipality. Many officials of the HCP are also destined for propaganda work and especially for the party schools. They, collectively, constitute "the apparatus," that is, the army of paid officials, the "permanents." In order to measure, if only by approximation, the numerical importance of this army, however, it is necessary to take into account the "false" volunteer activists: secretaries of middle-level organizations (cells) who are carried on the payroll of their respective companies but who work practically full-time for the party.

Thus about one communist in seven or eight is probably a party official.

The age groups differ from one period to the next, and the facts are not available for all periods. In 1948, before unification with the SDP, 18.9 percent of the members were under twenty-four years old, 63.6 percent were between twenty-four and fifty years, and the rest—roughly 18 percent—were older. Except for some minor fluctuations, these proportions have hardly changed. When the HCP was reorganized after the events of 1956, the ratio of the "old-timers"—CP members since 1945 or before—even increased in proportion to the MDP: 35 percent of the members were "old-timers," to say nothing of the hundreds of thousands of

persons between thirty and seventy years of age who had
adhered to the HCP after 1945, left it in the meantime, and
been readmitted to the MSzMP. Since 1957, the MSzMP
has certainly grown younger. It is necessary to wait for its
base of old militants to die out for it to turn over a new leaf,
but the tendency is now toward rejuvenation. Among the
200,000 new members admitted between 1970 and 1975,
44.1 percent are under twenty-six years old, 44.9 percent
between twenty-seven and thirty-nine years old, that is,
178,000 members on the whole, as compared to 12,000
members of more than forty years of age.

The MDP, under the direction of Rákosi, emphasized the
adherence of women to the party. In fact, in 1948, 30 percent of the members were women, which probably represents
a world record not only in the communist movement but also
in the life of political parties in general. The MSzMP has had
to be content with less: women make up only 26 percent of
its membership. This decrease corresponded to a certain political "demobilization" of women who had returned to their
homes since 1956.

Above all a workers' party, depository of the dictatorship
of the proletariat, the HCP has always made great efforts to
form a solid foundation among the working class. In 1919, it
had this foundation: social agitation reigned in Hungary as in
the rest of Europe, and it had merged with the SDP, which
brought all the unionized workers with it. During the long period of illegality, between 1919 and 1945, it was among the
workers of the lage factories in Budapest, Ujpest, Diósgyör,
among the miners of Tatabánya and Salgótarján, among certain metalworkers, leather workers, tailors, and others that
the HCP obtained certain successes. Other centers, such as
the big metallurgical center of Csepel—"red Csepel"—were
influenced by the communist factions that opposed the
official party line (e.g., the faction of Pál Demény) as well as
by the fascist extreme right. Everywhere, of course, the SDP
easily dominated the small communist groups in this respect.

Immediately after the war, on the other hand, the HCP gained much ground at the expense of the SDP. But the latter remained more firmly entrenched in the large factories of Budapest than its communist rival. In seven key factories, the HCP had 14,000 members in February 1946 and more than 38,000 after the unification. Certainly, part of this increase results from the successive mergers with the HCP, and another part results from the increase in the total number of workers. Nevertheless, between the two numbers, one perceives that the social democratic factor was indeed becoming weaker, though it was still powerful. It was the same throughout Hungary. Although weaker in the provinces, in January 1948, shortly before the unification, the SDP still had 290,000 members in the factories nationwide against a slightly higher number of communist workers.

There is another significant sign: in the purges after the unification of the two parties, an astonishingly high number of workers were excluded from the party, namely, 51,600, no less than 28.8 percent of all those excluded. More than 50,000 others were demoted to candidates. We have here, without any doubt, about 100,000 social democratic workers who were judged not trustworthy enough to be admitted to the HCP or to be admitted without a preliminary period of "candidacy."

The result was a paradoxical situation. The HCP before unification counted 34.7 percent factory workers and 6.6 percent agricultural workers; the unified HCP-MDP counted slightly less.

The statistics given in the HCP publications show a strong proportional increase of worker members for the years 1950-1953. About 130,000 factory workers are said to have joined the HCP during this period, raising to 50 percent, even to 59.2 percent for 1953, the proportion of the proletarian element in the party. In reality, however, those numbers were calculated by taking into consideration not only the profession that the counted members actually practised, but also

Table 3

	1951	1952	1953	1954	1955	1956
Percentage of workers according to their origin	56.9	57.1	59.2	60.5	58.9	58.0
Percentage of workers according to profession practiced	41.2	40.0	38.0	38.6	37.4	37.3
Percentage of workers according to industrial statistics	33.0	31.0	26.0			30.3

their social origin (Table 3), so that the communist worker who had become a minister of state or a general has the same statistical value as a former minister or a general turned worker. Owing to statistical checking, these official sources eventually admitted that by taking into account only the professional distribution, the proportion of workers, instead of growing, constantly diminished in the party: 41.2 percent in 1951, 40 percent in 1952, 38 percent in 1953, 38.6 percent in 1954, 37.4 percent in 1955, and 37.3 percent in 1956 (Table 3). The same source gives a still lower estimate obtained by comparing the party statistics with industrial statistics (Table 3).[5] The massive promotion of former workers to administrative posts and directorships (party, state, army, police, companies) was not solely responsible for this. The decline in the standard of living, the rise in the work norms, an oppressive political climate, and disillusionment and discouragement also played a role in it.

The HCP, reorganized after the events of 1956, seems to have shown a rather strong increase in the proportion of the miscellaneous categories, employees, peasants, and others, at the expense of the worker element. Or should previous statistics on workers have been established more scrupulously and more precisely? Be that as it may, *Legyözhetetlen erö* indicates that from February 1957 the criteria of computation have changed.[6] For the total proportion of workers in the party, our source gives about the same percentage for 1957 as for 1956, that is, 57.9 percent. For 1975 the *Proceedings of the XI Congress* gives 59.2 percent. On the other hand, in 1957 only 29.5 percent are workers occupied in production. In Table 3, to be sure, the 1956 figures also are much lower than before: 30.3 percent instead of 37.3 percent.[7] Have the new criteria already been applied retrospectively to arrive at this column? At any rate, starting with 1956-1957, the proportion of workers draws closer to the adjusted figures of the previous period—adjusted, as we have seen, according to industrial statistics—than to the official figures drawn from the party statistics before 1956.

From 29.5 percent in 1957, the proportion of workers increased to 34.6 percent in 1962 (177,315) and 35.1 percent in 1966 (204,731).

The proportion of peasants is 14-15 percent according to social origin, about 12 percent according to profession in the years 1950-1953, and about 10.5 percent between 1954 and 1956—a percentage that further decreases slightly in the following years. Workers and peasants together represented 46.8 percent in 1970 and 45.5 percent in 1975.

The figure for communist intellectuals shows an almost constant increase. From 4-6 percent in the 1950s, it reached 10.3 percent in 1962 and 11.9 percent in 1966.

The proportion in the miscellaneous category has also risen. It was 6-8 percent of the membership of the MDP before 1956 and 18-20 percent of the members of the MSzMP, without a significant change from 1957 until today. This rise is partially explained by the adoption of new census methods that are closer to reality. The MSzMP has separately enumerated its members serving in the armed forces, retired people, and other miscellaneous categories, which previously had been disguised in the statistics under more general headings. Other factors have also contributed to this rise of the "miscellaneous": for example, the natural increase in the number of retired persons (since the age limit was very low, communists who had joined the party in 1945, at the age of thirty-five or more, were already retired at the time of the Tenth Congress in 1970).

The number of retired persons is thus increasing and condemns the party to practically irremediable aging.

Besides the workers, the category of employees constitutes, as has always been the case, the main body of HCP membership: 34-39 percent in the 1950s, 28.7 percent in 1962, 26.1 percent in 1966—a progressive decrease probably due to changes in the statistical headings as well as to withdrawals.

The available facts concerning the composition of the HCP according to age, profession, and social composition are incomplete and contradictory. They are also based on changing and imprecise criteria. The authors of our principal source, *Legyözhetetlen erö,* frankly admit their own difficulties: for instance, the criteria to be adopted for the classification of workers in a society where, owing to modernization, the distinction between the physical worker and the technician or the organizer is more difficult to establish. In spite of the resulting uncertainties, the publications of the Hungarian CP furnish enough information to give a relatively clear idea of the composition of the party. What becomes evident is the tendency toward aging and at the same time the decreasing proportion of manual workers and peasants. Party officials, officers, retired persons, intellectuals, and the undefined miscellaneous categories constitute by far the majority of the membership: about 60 percent. According to the *Proceedings of the XI Congress,* this figure was even less in 1975, i.e., 54.4 percent. The aging of the party cadres may be natural, given the factors that have contributed to it, but the other factors are political. That is, they are a matter of policy, much like the massive promotion of communist workers to administrative posts and to directorships. Political factors also working against the will of the leaders and making the party less and less a workers' party—for example, the successive waves of disinterestedness on the part of the peasants, who left the party ranks en masse on various occasions. One fact is at first sight astonishing: according to repeated indications in the official sources, there are relatively more exclusions among peasants and workers than in other categories. In fact, the HCP has apparently attracted more lower-middle-class elements than proletarians. A simple worker often finds less to gain from his adherence to the party than an employee who desires to climb the social ladder, especially since the vast worker promotions have come to an end. Nor did the events of 1956 make the HCP more attractive to the workers. The factory workers were strongly attached to the ephemeral institutions of self-government in the framework of the workers' councils (see below), and they long opposed the establishment of the Kádár government. Their attitude seems to have changed much since then, but no factor has intervened to draw them into the ranks of the party. On the contrary, in spite of an undeniable amelioration in their standard of living, the workers often feel more economically disadvantaged than other segments of society, such as the peasantry, the artisans, and the small merchants, beneficiaries of an economic system that has sometimes allowed them a certain scope for their activity. On the other hand, the HCP attracted, after 1956, those sections of the population that had perceived the confusion of this year either as a true counterrevolution or as a warning laden with threats of all sorts. For party officials, a repetition of 1956 would have meant the loss of political and social status and of the advantages and privileges that go with it. For others, including the Jews, the revolution of 1956 cast the shadow of a past burdened with memories of the anti-Semitic campaigns and with a climate of uncertainty. Apart from political and ideological considerations, in short, the search for security pushed these social elements toward

Kádár's MSzMP, which offered them at one and the same time a policy that broke with the excesses of the Stalinist past and a continuity concerning the status of the political class.

Certainly, the present HCP, with its some 700,000 members, again resembles the party before 1956 more than it does the MSzMP of the first years after its reorganization. Purely existential motives must therefore have brought it a certain proportion of its present adherents. Nevertheless, the HCP-MSzMP is based on an important core of members who are devoted to its cause and who support it to a man. The relations between the leadership of the party and the mass of its members seem more intimate and closer than they were under Rákosi's Stalinist regime. At the same time, loyalty to the leadership requires less constraint today than previously. A Hungarian communist expresses himself more freely now than twenty years ago, he does not feel followed and watched even in his private life, and he allows himself a life-style that conforms to his personal tastes. Certainly, standards remain strict. But disciplinary punishments—to the point of exclusion in serious cases—also reflect a certain laxity, which the communists of Rákosi's era avoided lest even more draconian measures be imposed.

The comprehensive report of the Control Commission of the party, presented at the Ninth Congress in 1966, probably gives a faithful picture of the political, economic, and private manners of the Hungarian communists.

Between the Eighth and Ninth Congresses, the disciplinary commissions inflicted 26,227 punishments, of which 6,605 were exclusions. The Control Commission of the Central Committee was itself called upon to consider 1,755 cases: appeals, rehabilitation requests, and the like. It pronounced 243 exclusions.

The total number of exclusions was then relatively low: less than 7,000 in four years, as against 175,000 on the average in the MDP for an equivalent length of time.

The distribution of the offenses seems more significant. During the Stalinist period, exclusions and other punishments were pronounced almost solely because of the past or the political behavior of the accused. But the 26,000 or so punishments of the years 1962-1966 were distributed altogether differently. Foremost were punishments inflicted because of immoral behavior in private life: 6,806 cases in four years. Exactly 4,961 party members, of whom 1,435 were higher cadres or members of the armed forces, were punished for corruption or other "economic" offenses. Another 1,547 were punished for the nonexecution of party resolutions, and only 200 were punished because of "antiparty" activities and opinions. The nature, probably minor, of more than 10,000 disciplinary cases is not indicated in the report.

As is evident in these figures, specifically political punishments were relatively infrequent. The report specifies, moreover, that it was above all a question of dogmatic, sectarian opinions and activities: "Whereas middle-class, lower-middle-class, and right revisionist opinions manifested themselves essentially outside the party ranks, in the ranks of the members certain persons have tried to demoralize their entourage by their sectarian opinions. They have labeled the political leading line of the party as well as its leaders as 'revisionists.' Starting from pseudo-leftist dogmatic opinions, they have ended in anti-sovietism."[8]

Analysis of various sources and signs thus demonstrates, once more, that the leadership of the HCP, under János Kádár, had to confront opposition within the party, a "left" opposition composed essentially of sectarian elements as well as of a certain number of persons admitted to the reorganized party but cast out from the high offices they had held earlier.

Structure and Leadership

Apart from a few minor differences, the HCP is based on structures that are identical to those of other communist parties in power: basic cells in companies, administrative units, institutions, villages, or neighborhoods. The cells are part of broader territorial organizations, which are themselves placed under the authority of county committees in the provinces and city committees in urban areas. With the exception of the neighborhood or village cells, the basic organizations are found at the place of work; but on the higher levels the distribution is territorial and geographic. The basic organizations, in the factories of Budapest for instance, are placed under the authority of precinct commissions, which are in turn subordinate to the Greater Budapest Committee. In the provinces, the county committees are responsible for all the party organizations in their respective administrative units.

With the exception of political and electoral campaigns, demonstrations, and the like, the neighborhood cells have had neither great importance nor many tasks to fulfill. The cells in factories, ministries, and companies have had more, since they exercise a "leadership" function—always poorly defined—in the conduct of affairs at the institution itself: production, work discipline, salaries, moral climate, political information and propaganda. They have an identical role in the local union organizations as well as in the so-called mass transmission organizations, such as the councils of women and cultural organizations. The Young Communists, although they have a certain autonomy, also work under the direction of the party organizations, as we shall see.

The committees of five major cities and of the nineteen counties enjoy true political autonomy and power. Yet they, too, are subordinate to the Central Committee, the superior party organ between congresses. At times, especially in 1945-1953, the autonomy of the provincial committees alarmed even the central leadership. Certain county secretaries played the "petty prince," behaved as if they were new nobles, and allowed themselves to take no notice of the instructions sent out by the Central Committee. Today, this problem seems resolved, but the decision-making power of the city and county committees remains rather important with respect to local affairs.

The real political power is concentrated in the hands of the Central Committee and its apparatus, which is divided into departments (economy, propaganda, etc.). Elected by the party congress, which convenes every four years, the Central Committee is theoretically the embodiment of all members of the party and the executor of their collective will. In practice, however, it is something else again. Before 1956, the party congress assembled at irregular intervals: once during the Republic of the Councils in 1919, twice during the period of illegality (1925 and 1930), four times between 1945 and 1956 (1946, 1948, 1951, and 1954), four times between 1957 and 1970 (1959, 1962, 1966, 1970). (The numbering of the congresses dates from the first congress of the KMP, Party of the Communists of Hungary, in 1925.) The Eleventh Congress was held, with a little delay, in March 1975.

At present the delegates are elected to the congress according to the rules in effect since 1966. The Central Committee determines the number of delegates, and the conferences of the nineteen counties and the Budapest conference elect them. According to custom, the delegates are elected from lists presented by the territorial committee. Theoretically, indeed, the "great electors," assembled in conference, are free to modify the list, even to reject it and choose other candidates. In practice, however, they simply approve the list. Under these conditions, the mass of the members has no influence whatever on the composition of the congress.

The delegates thus assembled every four years as the general party congress amount to some 500-600 persons, selected according to a clever formula for age, sex, seniority, geographical, social, and professional distribution. The party congress is essentially a voting machine. It passes everything the leadership proposes: program, regulations, special resolutions, and, lastly, the new central committee. Consequently, the election of the latter is a matter of routine. The list is established in advance by the Politburo and the Central

Secretariat and is approved by an ad hoc Bureau for Candida-
cies. The voting is done without challenges. The official candidates are all elected, without exception. Whatever conflicts
there might be among tendencies, clienteles, or persons—they
do exist all the same—take place behind the scenes, never in
front of the congress, never in public. Those in power have,
with the help of this system, a whole series of safety valves.
They control the selection process at all levels. From the
delegates of the conferences to the delegates to the congress,
all electors are carefully selected, and at the same time, owing
to the system of official lists, any surprise is practically eliminated in advance. Changes against the wishes of the leading
group—to say nothing of reversals—can only occur in two
ways: either with the help of a genuine revolution within the
party or with "help" from abroad. The first has only happened once: in the summer of 1956, four months before the
revolution, the discontent of the "base" forced the Central
Committee to get rid of Rákosi with, it is true, the assent of
the Kremlin. The second is more frequent. In 1953-1954, for
example, the high party organs, first the Politburo and then
the Central Committee, were rather profoundly reorganized
on the pressing "recommendations" of the Presidium of the
Soviet CP, which was anxious to weaken the preponderant
influence of Rákosi's group.

Apart from this kind of reorganization, the team in
power is sole master of the situation. It never relinquishes its
power, which, in principle, it exercises by delegation, and it is
jealously on the watch to ensure that the statutory renewal
of the Central Committee by the congress—theoretically the
highest organ—is done according to what has been decided in
advance.

Thus elected by the congress, the Central Committee in
turn elects its Politburo as well as the members of the other
central organs: the Secretariat, commissions for propaganda,
economy, and the like. In the 1950s, the members of the
Organization Bureau (which no longer exists) were also nomi-

nated by the Central Committee; in contrast, the department heads of the party apparatus, who previously were simply appointed, are now elected by the Central Committee.

It would be easy to spell out these procedures in detail. But it is more difficult to answer the fundamental question of what is the actual power of the Central Committee? In theory, it is, and has always been, the party's highest decision-making organ between congresses. In reality, since the party came out of the underground, the Central Committee has never held the power nor played the role that the party constitution gives it. Since 1945, the Politburo has monopolized the seat of power, and the Central Committee has confined itself to approving the Politburo's decision.

This situation has subtly changed since 1953. Even if certain political adjustments and personal changes were imposed by Moscow, the Central Committee has become a battleground for fights over different views and has thereby assumed a certain importance. Between 1953 and 1956 in any case, it could—and this has happened once or twice—tip the scale to one side or the other. In October 1954, for instance, Imre Nagy prevailed over Rákosi thanks to the support of the majority of the Central Committee; a little over a year later, Rákosi was to win the victory in the same manner over his adversary. Similar situations have since occurred within the central committees of the MSzMP. In 1962, finding himself in a weak position in the Politburo, Kádár carried the debate before the Central Committee in order to be able to counter the campaign of the "dogmatics" against his policies of liberalization. Later, in the wake of these events, János Kádár undertook a sweeping reorganization of the Politburo; he eliminated successively Károly Kiss and György Marosán, and replaced Miklós Somogyi, Sándor Rónai, and Ferenc Münnich—retired in consideration of their age or deceased—with persons devoted to his politics. At the same time he strengthened the Central Secretariat. It is not impossible, however, that the present Central Committee supports

Kádár's politics less firmly and that the recent personal changes—for example, the semi-disgrace of Aczél and Nyers—correspond to a renewal of the Central Committee's vigor.

Certainly the Central Committee's inclinations toward independence have never had an altogether autonomous character. Moscow always had a hand in it. On the other hand, the Central Committee expresses primarily the climate of opinion that reigns among the apparatus, to which it is very close. Composed of about a hundred members, the Central Committee has about twenty-five ministers and deputy ministers, as many if not more high party functionaries, about twenty other high state and company officials, roughly fifteen officials from unions and other mass organizations, and about ten workers and intellectuals. It is, then, a body representing essentially the three great bureaucracies: the party, the state, and the mass organizations. It is not surprising that it is sensitive to the mood of the apparatus and that it tries to make the latter's opinion prevail. No leading communist team, not even a Stalin, would be able to govern without the assent of the high bureaucracy.

On the other hand, however, the Politburo is in a position to control all these bodies, as well as the Central Committee itself. It relies essentially upon the same party apparatus, which occupies a predominant place in the Central Committee and which, through the subtle play of the hierarchies, also dominates the state and union bureaucracies. We shall come back to this aspect of the question, but it should be remembered that the influence of the party apparatus extends well beyond its representation in the leading organs, because the various departments of the central party apparatus have a right to control, if not to decide, the affairs administered by state, union, and other bureaucracies. But relations between this apparatus, on the one hand, and the real leading team of the Politburo and of the Secretariat, on the other hand, grant the latter if not unlimited, at least unequalled power, the more so since it can also utilize, if necessary, the services of the political police. The apparatus, certainly, could not in the long run tolerate a Politburo and a Central Secretariat opposed to its interests, but at the same time it is devoted and loyal. Therefore, as long as the equilibrium in this subtle interdependency is not upset by a domestic overthrow or foreign intervention, the leading group of the party reigns over the apparatus, and the apparatus for its part ensures the leading group's supremacy in all the other party organs, including the Central Committee.

In short, one can affirm, without great risk of being wrong, that—contrary to the party congress, which practically never exercises its authority—the Central Committee can play an almost autonomous leading role, but only under extraordinary circumstances. But in "normal" times, and as long as it fulfills "heaven's mandate," the leading team of the party unquestionably has the real decision-making power.

To whom does "leading team" refer? Does it refer to all those who were placed in office, such as secretaries and members of the Politburo of the party? Or only to three or four persons whose names appear on the lists—or in any case appeared on the list—not in alphabetical order, but according to the place they occupy in the hierarchy? Or even to one man, as was allegedly the case with Stalin, or even Gottwald, Bierut, and Rákosi? For the Hungarian CP, it appears more appropriate to speak of duumvirate, triumvirate, or quadrumvirate than of the dictatorship of a single person. Mátyás Rákosi was certainly the sole and undisputed head of the party between 1945 and 1953. He, like most of his peers, was also the object of a "personality cult." According to a 1956 survey of the Hungarian section of Radio Free Europe, he gave his name to three streets, one university, two factories, thirty-one cooperatives, one scholarship, one school competition, one honorary decoration, one kindergarten, and one cultural center. His picture was on the walls of all offices, workshops, schools, and public halls in the country, and his biography was obligatory reading on all levels for all citizens between the ages of six and sixty. It seems, however, that among the leadership a certain division of powers existed. Ernö Gerö, as already stated, had an influence almost equal to that of Rákosi and seems to have been the *éminence grise* of the regime. Two other members of the Politburo also occupied choice positions: József Révai, responsible for and master of the vast domain of propaganda and cultural affairs, and Mihály Farkas, at first head of the Organization Bureau, later of the police and army section, and finally, for a brief period after Révai's withdrawal, of cultural affairs. True lieutenants of Stalin, chosen in Moscow well before their return to Hungary, these four men were without any doubt the HCP's "leading team" until 1953, but Rákosi and Gerö had more authority than the other two. The political police, for example, was officially put under the command of Farkas, but Rákosi nevertheless remained its real head, as he himself admitted in his "self-criticism" pronounced in 1956 in connection with the rehabilitation of László Rajk. The more shadowy role of Gerö has never been entirely elucidated, but numerous indications seem to prove his ascendancy over the political police, probably owing to his relations with the Soviet police services. As for Révai, he seems to have had in fact less real power than his colleagues. He is not known to have had any powerful connection in Moscow, and he did not endeavor to create for himself a "clientele" in the party apparatus. His friendship for László Rajk, executed in 1949, could not but hurt him. After 1949, his actual influence on the highest political decision making became considerably weaker.

In the group originally from Moscow, Imre Nagy still occupied a choice position between 1945 and 1948, but he was to be ousted rather quickly from the intimate circle of the "big four."

As for the other Muscovites who returned very early, they certainly held confidential and key positions: ministers such as Jószef Gábor and Zoltán Vas; heads of the army's political and intelligence departments, respectively, such as Sándor Nógrádi and Géza Révész; high functionaries such as Erzsébet Andics, István Friss, Ferenc Münnich, Béla Szántó, and Zoltán Szántó; those in charge of propaganda or questions of ideology, such as Georg Lukács, Béla Fogarasi, and László Rudas; or writers such as Andor Gábor, Béla Illés, and Sándor Gergely; as well as scores of others were not really assimilated into the all-powerful group of four.[9]

Numerous other members of the leading organs of the party were, at one time or another, as important as the ones just mentioned. This is the case for István Kossa, Imre Horváth, Andor Berei—all of them, moreover, also had Muscovite antecedents—as well as for Károly Olt, István Hidas, András Hegedüs, Arpád Kiss, Ferenc Nezvál, and Erik Molnár, all of whom were ministers or deputy ministers in a postwar cabinet. One could give many more examples. However, like the majority of the Muscovites who returned after the war, they were not associated, even if they were members of the Politburo, with the more intimate circle of the leaders.

Since there were leaders other than Rákosi, Gerö, Révai, Farkas, and (for two short periods) Imre Nagy, the group of the "interior leaders" must be examined from the very first. As has been seen, the latter in fact constituted itself as Provisional Central Committee in September 1944 and maintained itself as such until its unification with the other Central Committee; this in turn had been formed on November 5, 1944, in the eastern part of the country by Ernö Gerö, Imre Nagy, József Révai, and Mihály Farkas on their return from Moscow.

It would undoubtedly be exaggerated to speak of power struggles between these two central committees, but the group from the "interior" was nevertheless bent on preserving its position at the head of the party. Besides the Muscovites, another group of leaders thus emerged: Antal Apró, Márton Horváth, János Kádár, Gyula Kállai, Károly

Kiss, and István Kovács. Its younger members included
Ferenc Donáth, Géza Losonczy, and finally many ex-
servicemen from the Spanish Civil War. This group was
headed, after his return from German prisons, by László
Rajk, the last secretary of the illegal HCP. If he lost this title
to Rákosi at the time of the unification of the two central
committees, he was still an undersecretary and, of course, a
member of the Central Committee (the Politburo did not yet
exist) in the company of Apró, Horváth, Kiss, Kovács, Kállai,
Kossa, Kádár, and, of course, the Moscow group. Zoltán Vas,
who had also come from Moscow; Gábor Peter, the future
head of the political police; and Bertalan Barta also belonged
to this first unified, but provisional, Central Committee.

   In September-October 1946, the first congress held after
the war—the third party congress—legalized the existing situation and, at the same time, made important modifications.
Through the creation of the Politburo, the Central Committee, as already noted, yielded its decision-making power to
this new organ. At the same time, the Moscow group
strengthened its position. In fact, in the Politburo (established at the close of the Third Congress), the only members
of the interior group to recover their positions were János
Kádár, László Rajk, Antal Apró, and, half Muscovite, half
militant of the interior, István Kossa. The majority were
Muscovites: Farkas, Gerö, Nagy, Rákosi, and Révai. The
General Secretariat included Rákosi as first secretary, Farkas
and Kádár as deputies.

   This does not mean that the other notables of the interior
lost their influence. With a few exceptions, they are again
found in extremely important posts: Károly Kiss as president of the Control Commission, Márton Horváth as director
of the party newspaper *Szabad Nép,* István Kovács as department head in the Central Committee apparatus and later as
first secretary of the Greater Budapest Committee. After the
Politburo was expanded in 1951, they became members
along with some other cadres that had been promoted. By

then, however, neither the former social democrats nominated in 1948 on the occasion of the unification nor the best-known former militants of the underground period (Rajk, Kádár, and others) were on the scene. They had all been eliminated in the meantime by the purges: the social democrats, such as Szakasits, Marosán, Rónai, Vajda, and Révész were in prison; László Rajk had been executed; Kádár and Kállai were in prison; Kossa and others had been demoted. The only group to remain permanently in power was the four from Moscow. They fought no blood feuds among themselves. The only member of the group eliminated from high responsibilities was Imre Nagy. The others were watchful: at no moment did they let the relationship among the constituent groups of the highest organs vacillate. Between 1945 and 1948, they formed the majority in regard to the interior group. When they were compelled in 1948 to take some social democrats into the Politburo and Organization Bureau, they dismissed most of the non-Muscovite militants, only to take them back when positions again became vacant in the wake of purges and trials. This is not merely a question of maintaining a balance. In addition to the former socialists, Rajk, Kádár, Donáth, Losonczy, Szönyi, and others—the elite of the HCP of the interior—went to their graves or, at best, to jail. Those promoted in 1950-1953 were men of the second line. Rákosi and his peers did not need even to keep a majority so certain were they (with the aid of police terror, it is true) of the absolute docility of the Politburo. Thus, after 1949 and with still more reason between 1950 and 1953, the latter was reduced to mere technical tasks. As before, but with even more offhandedness, each important political decision was taken either by the permanent group of the four or by the General Secretariat directed by Rákosi, who shared his power only with Gerö and Farkas.

Have the modifications and the personal rearrangements that have occurred after 1953 really changed the power structures within the HCP?

Let us leave the role of the Central Committee behind. As for the Politburo and the Secretariat, they seem to have acquired—just as the Central Committee did—greater authority between 1953 and 1956. The partial retreat of Rákosi's group, which was imposed by the Presidium of the Soviet CP, gave free play to the confrontation of the "Rákosist" and "Nagyist" tendencies while favoring the appearance of a third, "centrist" tendency, which was to find its leader in the person of János Kádár after his reinstatement into the Politburo in July 1953, when Gerö replaced Rákosi at the head of the Central Secretariat. In a general way, the numerous adjustments of the leading party line, together with personal reshuffling, favored the renewal of the Politburo's importance. In it, some of the survivors of the purges met again, such as Kádár himself, Kállai, Marosán, and, in the days of revolution, Ferenc Donáth and Géza Losonczy; likewise, some militants of the old guard (such as Károly Kiss and Zoltán Szántó) and less-known persons (Ernö Ács and Rudolf Földvári) were reunited. Of the quadrumvirate, which the Kremlin practically dismissed in June 1953, Rákosi was to remain only until July 1956 and Gerö until the October Revolution of the same year; Farkas surfaced for a short period in the meantime. They definitely disappeared after the 1956 revolution. No other group was able to constitute itself, as had these four, as a restricted leading group. For a time, the Politburo shared power with the Central Committee, within the limits that have already been indicated.

What about the MSzMP, which took over in 1956 from the MDP? We have already mentioned the factional struggles among the leadership, struggles that led János Kádár to appeal to the Central Committee in order to reestablish the equilibrium in his favor in the Politburo. Except for these moments of crisis in the leadership, Kádár apparently had a solid base and a safe majority in the Politburo and in the Secretariat, which he directed. But he depended on the leading organs of the party more than his predecessors Gerö and Rákosi had done. He owed his power to several factors, among which was support from Moscow and from the apparatus, which as a whole seemed less devoted to him than it had been to the Stalinist leaders. This is only a hypothesis supported by certain telling indications. But if the indications that came to light along with the tensions and crises of the MSzMP are reliable, if there exists, despite the appearances of a firm, solid, and stable "Kádárist" leadership, a wavering and a plurality of powers, then how can one explain the longevity of this regime? János Kádár has maintained himself in power for twenty years despite all difficulties and despite the fact that he pursues a policy altogether unique in communist countries.

Should Kádár be seen as a neo-Stalinist leader relying upon the organs of coercion? Certainly not. Is he charismatic, then, a man whose talents and personality overcome each adversary? He does not appear to be that either. Everything leads one to think that there is a rather exceptional "Kádár phenomenon." One has to analyze his politics, his methods, and his personality in order to attempt to understand him, to explain at the same time the nature of a personal power that maintains itself despite a certain pluralism in the leading organs and bodies, which are not always and not necessarily favorable to him.

But before attempting this explanation, let us turn to the composition of the leading organs, their operation and their "driving belt," especially the so-called mass organizations.

The astonishingly copious and broad-minded information furnished by the official publications has depicted (see p. 65) a communist party that is shallowly rooted among the factory workers and even more shallowly among the peasantry. In order to prove that the party belongs to the working class —which is theoretically in power—party statistics refer us to the category of manual workers promoted to leading positions or, in the words of Djilas, to the bureaucratic "new class." In fact, most members of the leading organs are recruited there—Politburo, Secretariat, Control Commission, Commission for Revision, and Central Committee. If one reviews, as a significant example, the Central Committee of 1966, elected at the climax of the MSzMP but already after the Khrushchev era, this tendency is confirmed by the facts, at least apparently. This same Central Committee, according to the profession of its members, was apparently a typically bureaucratic organ composed of ministers, deputy ministers, department heads, secretaries of departmental committees, intellectuals, and of a handful of workers. If the same 101 persons are classified not by the profession actually practiced, but by original profession or social origin or both, however, the results are altogether different. The ministers and party notables become primarily peasants and workers: more precisely, fifty-two workers; ten agricultural workers, peasants, and gardeners; eight teachers, agronomists, and technicians; six miscellaneous employees; four writers and artists; and twenty-one engineers, professors, and other intellectuals. The Politburo has nearly the same proportions. From the point of view of their respective functions, we find four ministers, five high party officials, one director of the Historical Institute of the party, and one general secretary of the Union Council. From the point of view of their original profession, the same people are distributed as follows: six workers, one employee, and four intellectuals.

In certain cases, indeed, the "letters of proletarian nobility" are unreliable, but on the whole the breakdown reflects reality rather faithfully, more faithfully, in any case, than previous lists of this kind or lists published in the other communist parties.

For the sake of comparison, let us cite some data on the composition of the present Central Committee, elected in March 1975 by the Eleventh Party Congress. The new, enlarged Central Committee has 125 members. Of these, 81 seem to be workers or agricultural workers, as opposed to only 62 (52 workers and 10 agricultural workers) in the previous Central Committee. However, this seeming increase in the proportion of the workers is in fact an increase in the party bureaucracy. The number of workers who actually work in factories has not increased in the new Central Committee. At most, we can find six and, in addition, another six who are secretaries of factory cells of the party, most probably paid as officials and not as workers. Other "proletarian" members of the Central Committee include several company managers, trade union secretaries, first secretaries of the party in the precincts, ministers, under secretaries of state, army generals, and other high-ranking officials. For example, Kádár himself, the head of the state, the former president of the Council of Ministers, the president of the National Assembly, a deputy prime minister, two ambassadors, the president of the Broadcasting and Television Organization—all figure as proletarian members of the Central Committee. They were certainly workers once, but they stepped out of their overalls a long time ago. Under these circumstances, the increase of the worker–agricultural worker proportion does not mean very much.

In another sphere, the changes seem to be more significant (although it is rather difficult, for lack of information, to check them for accuracy), namely, the age and qualifications of the members of the Central Committee. As a result of the election of the new members, the Central Committee is younger and generally better educated. Party bureaucrats who lack culture or competence—although a few of them may be left over—belong to the past. Young officials have obtained their diplomas and endeavor to succeed, thanks to their know-how. The old apparatchikis so reminiscent of the past have gradually yielded their posts to this new bureaucracy, which is less reluctant than the old generation to accept Kádár's reforms and liberalism. The weight of the past remains, without any doubt, very strong, but the gradual metamorphosis of the party executives will probably show its effects in the not too distant future.

As for the operation of the party, the MSzMP, while giving a new content to its activities, does not formally differ from its predecessor. Likewise, its services resemble those of other communist parties in power. In theory, the party congress fulfills the role of "legislator"; the Central Committee directs the organization and activities between party congresses; the Politburo, which is responsible to the Central Committee, is the permanent executive; at its side are the Central Secretariat and, if necessary, other bureaus charged with such sectors as agitation and propaganda and the economy. As for the commissions of control and of revision, they fulfill special functions, particularly in the area of discipline and in the inspection of finances. Recently, they have been reunited into a single Control Commission, elected not by the Central Committee, but directly by the party congress.

According to the new party rules, the leadership is collegial, and the elected members are removable in the case of a grave fault. Decisions are transmitted on the principle of "democratic centralism," that is, resolutions taken by the higher organs are obligatory and executory for the lower organs. Likewise, each elected organ is responsible to the higher organ and must account for its activities. Discussion and criticism are authorized, even encouraged, as long as the majority has not taken a decision in the matter. However, the fundamental party statutes and resolutions no longer encourage, as they did in 1957-1960, members to participate in the elaboration of party politics. Likewise, the 1957 rules considered criticism a *duty* of each member and the stifling of criticism a punishable offense, but the new rules make this duty a simple *right*.

The organizations and cells (or basic organizations) were described above.

The Mass Organizations

According to a tradition that goes back to its origins, the

HCP has always made great efforts to create "mass organizations of transmission": organizations for the young, for women, for peasants, cultural, sporting, patriotic associations, and others. In addition, communist activity in the unions has always had capital importance. The nature of these organizations and their function, however, vary considerably from period to period.

During the underground phase between the two wars, the numerous organizations had above all to disguise HCP activities. Since the HCP was prohibited under the Horthy regime, the communists organized themselves and spread their propaganda among the unions, peasant associations, unemployed intellectuals, choral societies, athletic and nature clubs, and the like. The Young Communists have always had a particular, twofold "status": mass organization and semiautonomous organization of the party.

The politics of the popular fronts led to the creation of another kind of organization, for example, the Committee for Historical Commemoration and the Hungarian Front (embryo of the 1945 National Front for Independence). The March Front, which was created by left populist intellectuals in 1937, remained essentially populist, and finally was to terminate in the formation of the National Peasant party, which was rather close to the communists, but nevertheless independent. The Hungarian Front, founded later, deserves more attention from the point of view of HCP tactics. Through the Hungarian Front, the HCP in fact aimed at two more ambitious and more distant objectives than the mere utilization of the front as cover organization. From 1941 on, especially between 1942-1943, the HCP concentrated all its efforts on the formation of an antifascist democratic bloc. We have already mentioned some of the demonstrations that resulted from this. In 1943, after the dissolution of the HCP, the Békepárt [Peace party] pursued this policy with perhaps more élan and success, if only because of the reversal of the military situation on the Russian front. At any rate, the

Peace party succeeded in establishing contact with anti-German patriotic groups as well as in joining the common action of the SDP and the Party of the Smallholders. The latter wanted primarily to influence the regent Horthy and his entourage; the communists preferred to appeal to the masses. By means of the radicalization of the anti-German opposition, after the German army occupied Hungary on March 19, 1944, the conditions for a common front were ripe at last. The Hungarian Front was then born—with the participation of the social democrats, the left wing of the smallholders, the communists of the Peace party, and an anti-fascist religious organization, the League of the Lorrainese Cross. The National Peasant party was admitted later.

As the Red Army advanced, the political goal of this formation took shape. The question was no longer merely to organize resistance—which had a certain importance but which remained nevertheless a militarily negligible factor—but to prepare the postwar period. This period, certainly, was seen differently by different people. But they had points in common, especially the desire actively to participate in the postwar reconstruction. The putsch of the extreme right Arrow Cross movement and the collapse of the Horthy regime, after the regent's abortive attempt to reach an armistice, placed the Hungarian Front in the favorable position of a credible spokesman. At the end of November 1944, in fact, the parties of the Front, together with some other resistance groups, formed a Committee for Liberation and National Insurrection, under the presidency of Endre Bajcsy-Zsilinszky. Several general officers joined the committee in order to form a general staff for armed resistance. They fell into the hands of extreme rightist commandos, however, and perished just as Bajcsy-Zsilinszky had.

On the other side, the Soviets and the communist emissaries who came back from Moscow in the wagons of the Red Army had no great respect for the Hungarian Front and its Committee for Liberation. They instead chose their fellows, on the one hand, from other general officers of the Hungarian army who had passed over to the Russian side and, on the other hand, from the democratic political groups improvised in the liberated territories of eastern Hungary. On December 2, 1944, the communist general staff that had come from Moscow formed another front—National Front for Independence [of Hungary]; its composition was rather similar to that of the Hungarian Front.

At the end of 1944, then, there were two national fronts in Hungary, just as there were two central committees of the HCP. Urged on by the necessity to organize the postwar period—as early as possible and without waiting for the liberation of the capital—but also prompted by other considerations, the Muscovite communists, who had been parachuted into Hungary after an emigration that had lasted a quarter of a century, intended to organize the country according to the instructions they had received. But in Hungary as in the other countries of the region, the fronts were to play the same central political role. They were to constitute the vast framework for a political reconstruction; they allowed the HCP to exclude not only the rightist elements but also the liberal anticommunists and to assure the HCP itself of a position of strength. Thus the Yalta accords were respected to the letter while at the same time arrangements were made with a view to eventual changes.

The front still exists under the name of Patriotic Popular Front. During the past three decades, it has been reorganized and renamed several times. At a brief moment in its history, in 1954, Imre Nagy attempted to restore its original function of assembling the democratic forces, but he was not successful. The front, considered as a pluralistic organization, belongs to the era of the "beginning" of the people's democracies.

The other mass organizations have, to the same extent, lost the little autonomy that they had in the transition period of 1945-1948. They are numerous: National Association of

Cooperatives, National Council of Hungarian Women, Society
for the Propagation of Scientific Knowledge, National Peace
Council, Hungarian-Soviet Society, and others, not to mention the Young Communists, who remain, at the same time,
the most important organization and the reservoir of the
party. As "driving belts," their task is to spread the communist word in the circles they reach, then to "educate" as well
as "mobilize" these circles, if necessary.

Sluggish and bureaucratic, the unions have found a
renewed relative strength after the Kádárist reconstruction of
1957. However, their activities run counter to the inherent
limits of the state-as-employer system. Besides, they have
probably lost their credit among the workers, too. In this
respect, the events of 1956 are revealing. In this short period
during which free organizations blossomed, the unions did
not play a great part. The workers were instead trying to
form workers' councils, organs of production management
and local political power at one and the same time.

In order to understand the HCP's attitude toward the
council movement, it is necessary to state at once that the
latter has appeared and reappeared for half a century under
different names, not just under the label of councils or
soviets. In imitation of the Russian soviets, the Hungarians
formed workers', peasants', and soldiers' councils in 1918.
But in the bourgeois-democratic revolution of the end of
October as in the Republic of the Councils in 1919, the
political parties—first democratic, then social-communist
—got the upper hand, leaving to the councils only a
limited local field of action.[10] Nobody can say what would
have become of them had the commune survived. It is significant, however, that the HCP, which as early as 1919 and
against all common sense, adopted the slogan of a second
revolution and a second dictatorship of the proletariat—
just after the defeat of the first ones—did not insist in its
propaganda on the establishment of the councils. Certainly,
the illegal HCP's pamphlets and newspapers exalted the

"Tanácsmagyarország" (the "Hungary of the Councils"), but they never asked what concrete role the councils would play in the future as real holders of power in the dictatorship of the proletariat they envisioned.

At the end of 1944 and in 1945, Hungary was again the scene of a council movement. Encouraged by the communists, national committees constituted themselves in various localities as people's organs of power and administration. Simultaneously, factory committees were formed in various factories. Both were to disapppear. Undoubtedly, the democratic coalition parties, once established in power, were the first to oppose the preservation of the organs of self-government. For its part, however, the HCP defended them only timidly. It consented, after 1945, to regard the committees as bodies of political control and not administrative bodies. As a matter of fact, only the small National Peasant party envisaged a new type of state based on the people's organs of self-government. The HCP quickly gave preference to the reestablishment of the centralized state administration.[11] As early as January 10, 1945, József Révai asked in *Szabad Nép*, the HCP newspaper: "Are the national committees necessary, and for what purpose?" Yes, he answered in substance, the country needs the national committees as political organizations to fight for democracy, but not as administrative organs. "The national committees cannot undertake, must not undertake the tasks of local authorities (self-government) because they are political and not administrative organs." Consequently, it is not necessary, the article concluded, to recognize them legally. Years later, one historian concluded, "From April or May 1945, the operation of the national committees started slowly to go to ruin."[12] The factory committees survived the national committees. They were never organs of power; in the beginning, they served as support for the politics of the HCP not only against the employers but also against social democratic influence. After the nationalization of the factories and the absorption of the SDP, the

HCP no longer needed them. From the summer of 1947, the unions assumed control of the direction of the factory committees, which in 1948 were finally converted into union committees.

We have already mentioned the resurrection of the council movement in the Hungarian Revolution of 1956. This time, the workers' councils, in the factories, just as the local national councils, no longer only constituted themselves just to obtain power and to transfer it immediately to a government of one party or of a coalition of several parties. They wished to keep it in their hands altogether. The Soviet intervention put an end to the revolutionary experiments, and nobody can know what the final outcome of the political struggles would have been. But a government of the councils or at the very least a coalition government with the participation of the councils are possibilities that cannot be excluded. The HCP's attitude toward the council movement of 1956 had not changed. It looked on the emergence of the council movement with a poorly disguised hostility, and, after the Soviet intervention, Kádár's reconstructed HCP did likewise. For a brief time, Kádár still negotiated with the Central Workers' Council of Greater Budapest, but he did so only in order to gain time. As soon as the strength of his government was sufficiently consolidated, the workers' councils and the national councils were dissolved and their leaders thrown into prison.[13]

Before concluding this chapter on the structure, operation, and organization of the party, it is necessary to recall the role of the party apparatus in the administration of the state, the economy, and cultural life. Under one heading or another, all sectors of the state and even social domain are crowned by the departments or divisions of the central apparatus. At present, there are six: the departments for party affairs, propaganda, science and culture, economic affairs, public administration, and foreign affairs, not to mention the bureaus charged with the affairs of the Central Committee itself. They are "superministries"—either through direct intervention or through the intermediary of communists charged with high responsibilities in the state, union, and cultural bureaucracies, they control the operation of these organs. The intervention and control of the party apparatus is not always practiced at the same level or with the same intensity. Kádár's party has undoubtedly allowed the relations between the party apparatus and the state apparatus to become looser while conferring on the latter greater independence than during Rákosi's time. One must not, however, lose sight of the fact that the leading organs of the state—ministries, offices, and councils of every kind—are obliged to carry out the instructions of the party, i.e., the instructions of the Central Committee and Politburo. Consequently the party maintains its command over the state through the various channels of control and "transmission," even though the system has become more relaxed and less centralized than in the past.

3. The Communist Party and Its National Environment

Hungary

With a total area of 93,030 square kilometers and a population of 10 and a half million inhabitants, Hungary is one of the smallest of the medium-sized states of Central and Eastern Europe. It is also one of the oldest. The history of the Hungarian people and state goes back over a thousand years, among which were centuries of greatness and of power. Long linked to Austria through the personal union of the Habsburg sovereigns, Hungary before World War I was nearly three times larger than today and had a population of about twenty million inhabitants, almost half of whom were Slavs and Rumanians. After the Peace Conference and the Treaty of Trianon, all this changed completely. In post-Trianon Hungary, only insignificant pockets of nationalities could be found, with the exception of the German minority of Transdanubia. Most of the latter, however, were exiled after World War II. Consequently, present-day Hungary is not confronted with the problem of national minorities. On the other hand, more than three million Hungarians of the former kingdom remained, after 1919, in the "successor states," Czechoslovakia, Yugoslavia, and Rumania (enlarged by Transylvania). Here is the origin of Hungarian revisionism under Horthy between the two wars, a revisionism attenuated today, but probably not entirely resorbed.

Nearly two-thirds of the population belong to the Roman Catholic church and some 30 percent to the Protestant churches. The Orthodox and Jews are numerically of little importance. In prewar Hungary the Jews made up about 5-6 percent of the population (6.2 percent after World War I, 5.1 percent in 1930 not counting converted Jews). According to a recent book, only some 140,000 survived the Nazi persecutions, although its author estimates the present number at 100,000.[1] Actually, figures on religion in postwar Hungary must be taken with caution because individuals no longer declare their confession. In our estimate, at least half the 500,000 Jews of prewar Hungary are still in the country. The antagonism between Catholics and Protestants has long been a thing of the past. On the other hand, there is still a "Jewish question"—a latent anti-Semitism, especially toward the Jewish component of the HCP.

The population density is very high in the capital, which has almost two million inhabitants, and in some other urban centers. It varies between forty and one hundred per square kilometer in the agricultural regions.

An agricultural country in the past, Hungary is poor in minerals and energy resources. Yet certain sectors—machinery and transportation, mechanics, optics, food, chemical products, and textiles—experienced a rapid development even between the two wars. But about 56 percent of the population still lived from agriculture. A thousand landowners (1,070) possessed estates of over 575 hectares: altogether 2.6 million hectares, or almost 30 percent of the cultivable land. With about 11,000 other landowners possessing each estates of between 57.5 and 575 hectares, 12,064 landed proprietors held 4,338,000 hectares or 48 percent of the land. About 1,622,000 peasants shared the other half, or 52 percent.

The destruction during the war has been estimated at five times the annual national revenue. Therefore, the first economic plan essentially aimed at reconstruction. But from 1949-1950 the politics of industrialization began. In the meantime, two socioeconomic changes upset the countryside. In 1945 the new government, under pressure from communists and agrarians of the left, carried out a land reform that had long been awaited by the agricultural workers and the poor peasants. Exactly 642,342 people were allotted 1,875,000 hectares of land—2.92 hectares per person on the average. Simultaneously, the new state expropriated more than 1.3 million hectares of woodland, pastures, and uncultivated land. On the whole, in round numbers, 3,200,000 hectares of cultivable land were affected. Only in exceptional cases (war crimes, membership in the *Volksbund*) did the reform affect estates of less than 57 hectares. With one blow, seignorial, or "semifeudal," Hungary disappeared; it gave way to the new agrarian structures of small and medium landowners. In 1949, about 25 percent of the peasant farms were between 0.57 and 1.72 hectares, 21 percent between 1.72 and 2.87 hectares, 32 percent between 2.87 and 5.75 hectares, 17 percent between 5.75 and 11.50 hectares, and 6 percent between 11.50 and 57.5 hectares. These new agrarian structures were to disappear in the wake of the second great change: the collectivization of agriculture after 1949.[2]

The combined effects of industrialization, urbanization, and agrarian transformation have thoroughly changed the structure of the population and of the economy. About 23 percent of the population continues to live from agriculture, which provides some 18 percent of the national gross revenue. The share of industry has risen to 55 percent, and that of commerce and transportation to 22 percent. Besides Budapest, five cities have over 100,000 inhabitants (Miskolc, Debrecen, Pécs, Szeged, Györ), and twelve more have over 50,000.[3]

It is impossible here to trace the development of all the different sectors of the Hungarian economy. According to all available information, the prewar level of industrial production was reached around 1949-1950 and is said to have increased five times over by 1968 (the beginning of the economic reforms). It has grown since then at an average yearly rate of 6.3 percent. Agricultural production, too, is claimed to have achieved a high growth rate in proportion to the other socialist countries, namely, 5 percent yearly. The national income also has a high growth rate: it tripled between 1950 and 1968 and since the economic reforms has increased by about 7-8 percent yearly (1938: 100—1974: 483). According to a recent study (calculated using the value of the 1960 dollar), the per capita national income was $1160 in 1975. The average salary in industry is 2,700-2,900 florins monthly, that is, $108-116 at the average exchange rate of $1 = 25 florins. The purchasing power is much higher, however, because of low rents and inexpensive basic products and social loans.[4] It is extremely risky to compare standards of living. But it is certain that the real income of the Hungarian wage earners has increased considerably over 1950 and consequently over the prewar period. According to official statistics, the 1974 real income was 226 percent of that of 1960 and 134.5 percent of that of 1965. The standard of living of the workers, as well as that of the peasants, artisans, and intellectuals, has improved particularly since the introduction of economic reforms in 1968, although it remains inferior to that of East Germany and far below that of the Western countries.

According to a 1966 study of the Central Office for Statistics[5] (based on information from 15,000 households in 1963), the income range was not very large. Since there are no recent statistical studies as extensive as the one of 1966, there is no way to indicate the present income scale. However, the scale has apparently widened considerably in the wake of the rationalizations brought about in the economic reforms from 1968 to the present.

The stratification of the Hungarian society has constantly been changing since 1945 and, with still more reason, since the HCP was established as the only party in power. With the collapse of the prewar regime, a whole political and economic class disappeared, a class that had been firmly entrenched as the leading class. It is wrong to view it as an essentially aristocratic class based on its great landed properties, which survived in Hungary until 1945 and which in fact extended over half of the cultivated land. In reality, these high aristocratic classes and the nobility were retreating before the bourgeoisie or, very often, were intermingled with it. If the descendants of the great established families still dominated the Upper House of Parliament, the diplomacy, the army, and perhaps a few other privileged functions, they did not dominate economic and cultural life, public administration, or even political life. In all these vital domains, the "Christian and seignorial" upper middle class ruled as masters—with an assimilated Jewish bourgeoisie at its side.[6]

For some time after the war, it would still have been possible to follow this formerly dominant middle class as it went into full decline. The land reform uprooted one of its layers, the nationalization of the companies uprooted another, the purge of public administration a third, and so on. The political retreat of this class kept pace with its economic and social retreat. It was still an opposition during 1945-1948, but it then collapsed in total disintegration. The particularly odious police and administrative measures that the Rákosi regime took against its survivors between 1950 and 1953—suppression of retirement pensions, eviction, banishment from Budapest, and deportations—only affected elements that had become inoffensive and in general aged. In any case, the alleged "reaction" during the revolution of 1956 would not have had a social basis worthy of the name. Since then, the remnants of the former leading middle classes have disappeared, either by the assimilation of the young ones, or by the death of the older ones, or even by the exodus of 200,000 Hungarians to the West in 1956.

Communist societies have a special character, and it is not easy to define the new social structures. The peasantry, which, owing to the land reform, could have constituted, together with the former middle peasants, a vast rural lower middle class, has disintegrated, too, in the wake of the collectivization of agriculture. Modernization did the rest by reducing the agricultural population as a whole. The peasantry was formerly dispersed over the countryside on its small plots of land; at the same time, it was divided according to wealth. But today it is a more or less cohesive and uniform class concentrated in 2,000 agricultural cooperatives and 150 state farms. It makes up, as already stated, only about 23 percent of the population, including what remains of the individual farms and the wage earners of the state farms (16 percent of the agricultural population).

In absolute terms, the number of workers in agriculture (not counting the nonworking members of families) was 2,200,000 in 1949, 1,925,000 in 1960, and 1,487,000 in 1968, that is, 29-30 percent of the entire active population. Since 1968, this number has decreased further and fallen to about 800,000 in the agricultural cooperatives, to which must be added some 100,000 individual farmers and 160,000-170,000 wage earners in the state farms—or 1,060,000-1,080,000 on the whole. In other words, the rural exodus will soon have involved one million active workers. About 700,000 farmers left the soil between 1949 and 1968, some tens of thousands had already left it before, and more than 100,000 have done so since then. They have reappeared in other sectors of the economy, just as the individual artisans, who are now reduced to about 50,000, joined together with 200,000 more artisans in cooperatives.[7]

The vast majority of the active population are wage earners: officials of the administration, company employees, teachers, workers, and the like. The liberal professions are practically nonexistent, since almost all scholars, physicians, architects, lawyers, actors, journalists, and even writers work in state institutes, state hospitals, state offices, and state publishing firms. On the whole, they represent three and a half million wage earners, according to the latest available figures.

Hungary's ethnic composition, as already noted, is remarkably homogeneous. Owing to a generous policy toward the small groups of national minorities—Germans, Serbians, Croats, Rumanians—the relations of the authorities with them do not present any problem (except those that are specific to the social groups to which they at the same time belong).

It seems more difficult to gauge the importance of religion in the relations between the population and the authorities. The latter's policy toward the churches is actually very tolerant, which contrasts with the anticlerical and antireligious violence of the 1950s (see below on the crises and conflicts of the party). This tolerance is rewarded by a kind of political consensus, practiced by the Protestant churches as well as by the Catholics and Jews. To what degree does this consensus extend to the congregation of these churches? This we cannot answer: we do not know the proportion of those who attend church and, with still more reason, we do not know how many believe but do not attend church. Whatever the answer, it is clear that religious faith has ceased to be an important political factor. Even the invisible barrier between the Christian and Jewish faith on the one side and the communist doctrine on the other side is becoming less insurmountable than previously. As the practice of religion is free, a believer today can approve of the regime without coming into conflict with his own conscience. Moreover, if only in order to conform to social custom, many registered communists have their children baptized, even though they do not later send them to religious training. Party newspapers and pamphlets condemn such behavior, but it does not entail disciplinary measures for the culprits. Since the party uses only ideological means against the religions, the opposition stops at that; as before, neither side assumes a properly political character.

The domain of political feelings, sympathies, and antagonisms as well as the scale of values are, if that is possible, even more impenetrable than the problem of religious behavior. In the absence of free elections, an independent press and other mass media, impartial sociological investigations, and public opinion polls on a large scale, it is impossible to go beyond general estimates. It is especially difficult to determine the changes that have occurred since the 1956 revolution. This event well demonstrated the hostility of the population, if not toward socialism and some of its economic and social accomplishments, but in any case toward the communist political system. Certainly, there were no elections in October 1956 that could give any indication about the political preferences of the population. But in any case, very few would have voted communist: some 5-6 percent perhaps, in the estimate of such well-placed personalities as János Kádár and Georg Lukács.[8] The vast majority of Hungarians was divided between the political parties that had risen again, including the Catholic parties, and the tendency toward the council movement. This does not at all mean that cultural and moral feelings and values in favor of the past, conservative or reactionary, would have prevailed in Hungary in 1956. The deepest convictions of the population were expressed essentially in the rejection of the communist system, in its negation, not in the positive affirmation of other values and convictions. This was a negation of the monolithic system, a negation of the methods of totalitarian dictatorship, a negation above all of foreign influence, that is, of Soviet domination. This negation to a cetain extent implies the affirmation of opposite values such as nationalism, pluralism, and attachment to individual liberties. But for us to maintain that in revolution the Hungarian people had "voted" either for a parliamentary regime of the Western type, or for a system of councils and of self-government, would be pure speculation. The "plebiscite through revolt" of 1956 allows one to affirm only three things: (1) Hungarian nationalism manifested itself with extreme vigor against the Soviets;

(2) the communist system was clearly rejected on the political level; this does not necessarily imply the rejection of the new economic and social structures; (3) ten years of communist indoctrination had by no means erased the attachment of the population to liberal-democratic values.

More than twenty years after the events of 1956, it is difficult to measure present feelings. It remains unlikely, however, that either time or the undoubtedly more flexible and more liberal policy of the Kádár regime has changed the deepest convictions of the population. The positive consensus that the present regime enjoys rests, it seems, on well-defined economic and political bases, but by no means on new values and feelings. Hungarians follow Kádár's HCP, even support it to a certain point, as a lesser evil than the Stalinist past, as a lesser evil than the other communist regimes. They support the new economic policy, they support the sensible alleviation of the police system, they support the relative freedom the intellectuals enjoy, and they support the rather easy grant of passports. But they remain opposed to the single party system, to the Warsaw Pact and the presence of the Soviets in Hungary, to the disadvantages of the trade with the Comecon countries, and many others. In a word, the attachment to the nation, to pluralism and to liberal values remains intact, according to all available signs.

The Hungarian attitude toward imperialism—according to the same signs and uncertain estimations—is ambiguous. The ardent antiimperialism that communist papers report is probably found only in a thin layer of the population close to the HCP: members of the apparatus, privileged members of the state bureaucracy and the mass organizations, the political police—the army being already less certain on this point. On the other hand, the image of the West—of a "liberating" West in any case—has become tarnished considerably since 1956. Hungarians are no longer too optimistic about the Western powers, including the United States, as "champions of freedom." At the same time, the crusades, wars, and inter-

ventions of these powers in Asia and Latin America seem to
have provoked mixed feelings. Hungarians certainly did not
applaud the Vietnam War, especially not the human suffering
it caused, but at the same time they saw it as another proof
of the absence of determination in American policy. The
United States, it seems, has ceased to exert—for often contradictory reasons by the way—an attraction on Hungarian
opinion. It is not very probable that Mr. Nixon would have
received the same warm popular welcome in Budapest as he
did in Bucharest.

If Hungarian opinion seemed indifferent to, rather than
interested in, Vietnam (just as it is toward Cuba and Chile),
the same does not apply to the conflict in the Middle East.
Everything seems to indicate that public opinion sympathizes
with Israel. One cannot explain these sympathies solely by
Jewish influence in Hungary itself; after all, Hungary has a
solid anti-Semitic tradition. Nor can one explain them by
some anti-Arab racism. The principal factor in the
Hungarians' pro-Israel feeling lies in the fact that they regard
the conflict as a small people's struggle for existence against
the Arab countries supported by the Soviet Union.

The Soviet element, then, appears to be omnipresent in
the formation of public opinion. It determines behavior and
modifies even the scale of values. To understand its impact,
one has to keep in mind the importance of the Soviet presence
for thirty years, Moscow's direct role in the communist
seizure of power and in the crushing of the revolution, the
effect of "russification," as well as the difference between
the two cultures. The Hungarian perceives himself as emi-
nently European in his history, his religion, and his civiliza-
tion. The Soviet domination consequently is alien to him in
this respect as well.

In this respect, too, one must mention the dislike for the
Rumanians. If Hungarian nationalism has weakened toward
its other neighbors, the Yugoslavs and the Czechoslovaks, the
same is not true for its neighbors to the east. Hungarian

public opinion has always resented the separation of Transylvania more than it resented the loss of regions in the north and in the south given to Czechoslovakia and Yugoslavia, respectively. This resentment has remained alive even after World War II, particularly because of Rumanian policy toward the Hungarian minority.

Strategies and Tactics

The strategy and tactics of the HCP compared to those of other political parties have this peculiarity: "conflict" has an infinitely more important place than "integration." This does not mean that the HCP turns up its nose at the aspirations specific to its national environment. It takes them into consideration before as well as after the seizure of power. As we shall see, the national factor was of prime importance in Imre Nagy's experiment in 1953-1954 as well as in the more recent and more enduring one of János Kádár. But in the meantime, it is necessary to make some preliminary observations about the conflicts of the HCP.

During the long period in the underground after the failure of the Republic of the Councils in 1919, the HCP did not change its strategic line before the second half, even the end of the 1930s. It remained fixed on the final objective: the seizure of power by means of a proletarian revolution and, at the close of this revolution, the establishment of the dictatorship of the proletariat. Its main slogan was "For the second Republic of the Councils!" Considering the HCP's extremely limited audience, such a program was at one and the same time chimerical and heavy with threat. It appealed to forces that one could not even qualify as political minority groups, much less as social groups. The HCP simply tried to reach, through its propaganda and its organizations, the most disadvantaged, the most desperate, the most radical, the most exalted—but also the most idealistic people, those most ready to sacrifice themselves—in all social groups: workers, poor peasants, the unemployed, the sick, those on the fringes of society, disillusioned sons of the upper bourgeoisie, artists, students, and Jews. In the same spirit, it tried to enlarge this circle during the crises, which hit precisely the most wretched the hardest. Thus, while its program remained a chimera in interwar Hungary, the HCP envisaged the use of violence by small groups, which would attempt to impose their will on the majority of the population. In short, it envisaged the repetition of Lenin's coup of November 1917, but in entirely different conditions.

The violent and desperate character of these tactics and of the strategic objective at which they aimed was accentuated by other elements. First, the HCP did not represent any social class or any true social stratum. Consequently, it was not coherent enough to lead a struggle both social and political. Perhaps organized but by no means structured, the HCP called to the struggle groups that were even less structured, groups that changed at the whim of circumstances, amorphous and ephemeral.

Another factor that provoked the reckless violence of the HCP was its illegality and the police repression directed against it. According to François Fejtö's apt definition, the Leninist party is a kind of "counter-police" driven to use the very methods that the official police use against it.[9] One knows the consequences of this heritage in the politics of the HCP after the seizure of power; we shall come back to it. Meanwhile, let us add that the dynamics specific to small groups and small minority units also acted in favor of violence in tactics.

The appeal to active and determined small groups has proved to be more efficient, although still in a very limited way, since the middle of the 1930s. Owing to the tactics of the popular fronts, all communist parties, whether small or more important, were able to associate themselves with popular movements and wider, though minority, antifascist ideas. Ever since then, the call for violence had a goal other than the repetition of Lenin's achievement; it assumed a national character. All the same, it took almost ten years for the HCP to benefit from this change in tactics, which was of course imposed by the Comintern. The first obstacle was the very character of the HCP: its past, its traditions, its leaders, its composition. More than its brother parties, the CP of Hungary was imbued with its exalted past of 1919: it could not conceive of adopting a tactic "inferior" to the one that had made its glory at the time of the Republic of the Councils, a dictatorship of the proletariat. After this glorious past, to fight for a kind of democratic republic of the 1918 type was to go back an entire historical stage. Besides, the most prestigious of its leaders, Béla Kun, was also the least prepared to bring himself to it. Kun, as a matter of fact, was never capable of drawing the lesson from the failure of the Republic of the Councils of Hungary. On one level, it is true, Kun saw more clearly than many of his detractors. He knew very well that without associating themselves with the social democrats, the Hungarian communists could do nothing. But at the same time, he remained deeply attached to the tactics of violence as well as to the strategic goal of the proletarian dictatorship. The role he played in the Comintern, particularly in the attempted communist putsch of March 1921 in Germany, reveal the "Blanquist" adventurer in him. On the other hand, as his written works attest, Kun firmly remained with his 1919 positions during all the polemics and factional fights within the HCP through the 1920s. Finally, the works published by the HCP before and after Kun's rehabilitation reveal that even in 1936 "he had trouble breaking with the sectarian ideas of former times, and he curbed the necessary readaptations" of party politics.[10] This did not last long, it is true, because the GPU got rid of Kun, the hero who had become annoying. But, with Landler already dead in 1928 and Kun liquidated in 1936, the HCP no longer had a leader or a program (no more than it had a genuine social base) to help it adapt to the circumstances. Lukács's proposals—the Blum Theses—could undoubtedly have been a new starting point. But they were buried in the archives as well as in memories conditioned by terror. It is not customary in the party to come back to officially discredited theses, even if time did them justice. Lukács had to wait until 1956 before revealing that as early as 1929 he had advocated the policy of the "democratic dictatorship," a policy taken up again by the party first at the time of the antifascist fronts and later in the transition period from 1945 to 1948. Moreover, even if it had been possible, Lukács would not have been in a good position during 1935-1941 to launch his own arguments again. Therefore what little progress the HCP made toward an antifascist and democratic front came from the Prague-based Committee Abroad. Its newspaper *Dolgozók lapja* [Workers' journal] published the first rough drafts of the new policy, penned primarily by József Révai and István Friss.

This is not the place to follow the debates among Hungarian communists about the policy of the fronts and about the class relations to which this policy had to adapt.[11] As for the obstacles to its application, the least of which was not the dissolution of the party in 1936 by the Comintern and its difficult recovery, the matter has already been treated in the historical part of our study. Likewise, after August 1939, the German-Soviet Pact obstructed, obviously, all possibilities for an antifascist popular front until Hitler declared war on his former ally in 1941. Communist authors certainly try to blot out these "difficulties," but even a historian as discreet about errors as Agnes Ságvári eventually acknowledges that the elaboration of the new frontist politics "took years"[12] and that everything did not go smoothly.[13]

Despite some progress between 1937 and 1939, only after 1941 did the HCP really start to advance on the new path. In a resolution of September 1, 1941, "the Central Committee invites the leadership of the party to establish contact with the important bourgeois parties of Hungary, among others with the leadership of the government party in power, in the interest of the accomplishment of anti-German national unity."[14] It also invited the bourgeois parties "not to treat the communist party as an enemy but on the contrary as an ally." In return, the HCP promised not to transgress, for as long as the proposed alliance lasts, "the limits of the constitution" nor to attempt "to change by the use of violence the existing state and social order." "The Party of the Communists of Hungary," one further reads, "will use all its activity, its influence among the masses, and its organizational strength exclusively against the common enemy as long as the common national objectives have not been reached."[15]

This document refers to previous resolutions, especially those of October 3, 1940, and April 2, 1941, which are said to have been formulated in the same spirit. However, the existence of these resolutions has not been proved.[16] Be that as it may, the resolution of September 1941 was a beginning, although a slow and difficult one. We have pointed out the most important stages in the politics of the fronts as well as the duality between the initiatives taken "on site" in Hungary on the one side and in Moscow on the other side. The emissaries sent directly from Moscow (e.g., Zoltán Schönherz) actually directed the new politics; later, Ferenc Rózsa, Endre Ságvári, Gyula Kállai, János Kádár, László Rajk, Ferenc Donáth, and other militants of the interior resumed these politics. The duality, however, continued: as already noted, a Hungarian Front established in the country existed alongside a National Front for Independence founded by the Moscow group.

In Moscow, too, the policies of the fronts more and more assumed—as the Red Army advanced toward Hungary— the character of a "provisional power" for the postwar period. Radio Kossuth broadcasts from Moscow and later from less remote stations invited the parties and the antifascist and democratic forces to organize this political postwar period at the same time as they organized resistance against the Germans and the Hungarian extreme Right. In the Soviet Union, too, the émigré Hungarian communists feverishly organized "antifascist schools" in order to turn Hungarian prisoners-of-war into underground fighters and form future political and administrative cadres. Finally, it was in Moscow that the communist leaders and the officers and generals who made up the armistice delegation of the Hungarian army concluded the first agreements about the establishment of a provisional government. The tactics of the fronts in its broader first version consequently extended not only to democratic elements opposed to the Horthy regime, such as the social democrats and the smallholders, but also to these representatives of the anti-German wing of the traditional Right. This widened front did not last long: generals Béla Dálnoki Miklós, president of the Council of Ministers; János Vörös, minister of national defense; and Gábor Faraghó, minister of food; as well as Count Géza Teleki, minister of education, soon had to give up their respective posts to representatives of the democratic parties of the National Front for Indpendence.

The politics of the fronts thus took its "definitive" form for the transition years 1945-1948. The relation of forces was constantly modified in favor of the HCP owing to the "salami tactic," which consisted in eliminating adversaries slice by slice. The framework, however, remained unchanged. On the surface, tactics and strategy overlapped: the HCP affirmed, during all these years, that its only objective was a "free, democratic, and independent Hungary," in other words, a "new democracy" or a "people's democracy" headed by a government of all the united democratic forces. The HCP thus seemed to be a loyal partner in the realization of a far-reaching national project but not at all revolutionary in the proletarian Marxist-Leninist sense. For three years the words *dictatorship of the proletariat* were not even pronounced, and party spokesmen, especially Mátyás Rákosi, did not cease to severely criticize the "former sectarian comrades" who were nostalgic for the Republic of the Councils of 1919. For the errors and excesses of the latter, Béla Kun and "his com-

panions" were held responsible—a solution all the more convenient, since Kun had already been resting for almost ten
years in a common grave of the GPU prisons as well as in the
moral tomb of the "deviationists" condemned by the Comintern and Stalin in person. In short, Rákosi's HCP kept its
distance, that is the least one can say, from sectarianism of
any kind—an equally convenient solution, which permitted
no distinctions to be made among Kun and his supernumer-
aries, the faction leaders of the illegal HCP (e.g., Pál Demény
and Aladár Weiszhaus), the disappeared suspects of the International Brigades of the Spanish war, the "deviationists" of
the underground HCP, and all kinds of victims of the Moscow
purges. We shall come back later on to this immense collective tomb, which contains almost the entire past of the HCP
with the exception of a handful of survivors.

From the point of view of tactics, the HCP took other
measures to polish its new image. As promoter of the land
reform, it gave the illusion of a definitive democratic solution
for the agrarian problem by brandishing the slogan, "the land
to the peasants." Whoever talked of collectivization or
nationalization of the land was immediately accused as
"leftist," as "sectarian." On the cultural level, Georg Lukács
was brought forward. The party let him play the "pope" of
literature, a pope who was certainly rather dogmatic in the
eyes of writers living in their own poetic universe and thereby insensitive to the appeals for the construction of a new
society, but a "pope" who was astonishingly liberal and comprehensive in comparison to the Zhdanovs or even the
Bertolt Brechts. Lukács's cultural "platform"—thoroughly
supported by József Révai—admirably complemented the
general politics of the HCP and in fact was an integral part of
it. After all, in Hungary more than elsewhere, politics and
cultural life were intimately connected, even inseparable, by
tradition. A policy that appealed to the vital forces of the
nation would have had no credit if it had not been complemented by an analogous cultural program. Referring to the

great literary traditions, the party invited all artists, writers, scholars, and intellectuals to follow the example of Petöfi, Ady, and Attila József rather than that of the "ivory tower" artists.[17]

As for national traditions, no one exalted them as much, no one would have dared to exalt them in the presence of the Soviet Army, the heroes of the fight for Hungarian independence, as did the leaders of the HCP. The "new Hungary" and its "new democracy" appeared in their writings and their speeches as the direct continuation of the national insurrection of Prince Rákóczi and of Kossuth's war of independence. If we are to trust them, the wind of "1848" blew over Hungary, not the wind from the east.

This national frontist policy—tinged by a bit of genuine nationalism—also included the HCP's great, original project for the formation of new elites. That is, it set up a system of people's colleges to favor the promotion not only of young worker and peasant cadres but also those of bourgeois origins —in an essentially democratic and national spirit. In these colleges, crowned by the NEKOSz [National League of People's Colleges] and patronized by the communist minister of the interior, László Rajk, nothing was criticized with as much vigor as sectarianism and all other "left" deviationism.

It is neither possible nor desirable to survey how the HCP's new tactics were applied in all the domains of national life. Nor is it the place to give an account of the parallel movement, which consisted in weakening not only the Right, outside the front, but also the HCP's partners within the government coalition. Besides, the "salami tactics" are sufficiently well known to excuse us from recounting all the political maneuvers, voting frauds, intimidations, threats, and arrests. The political police, led by Gábor Péter and placed under the authority of the minister of the interior, László Rajk, soon extended its operation beyond the pursuit of war criminals, fascists, and harmful reactionaries. It became the HCP's political instrument against its own allies, if only by virtue of the threat—often carried out by the way—that it made to politicians little inclined to yield to the demands of the communists. Officials not protected by parliamentary immunity quickly got acquainted with the prisons of the AVO and later of the AVH [State Security Section, later State Security Authority] as well as with its notorious methods of interrogation. But in extreme cases, the HCP did not hesitate to appeal to the Soviet occupation authorities. In fact, the Soviet military police carried out the arrest of the secretary general of the Independent Party of the Smallholders, Béla Kovács.

Apart from pressure and intimidation, the HCP also made use of the masses. With the help of its disciplined and perfectly efficient organization, it succeeded in mobilizing many, many people, especially in Budapest. In the demonstrations against the "speculators and stockjobbers," and then in the demonstrations against "the reaction"—organized by the way under the insignia of the Leftist Bloc, an improvised formation whose purpose was to counterbalance the influence of the majority party of the smallholders—there were easily 100,000 persons, if not more.[18]

The HCP's policies toward the churches were also marked by a combination of moderation and violence. At first, the HCP energetically resisted the anticlerical and atheistic traditions of the old days. Mátyás Rákosi, secretary general of the HCP, had his picture taken at baptisms and accepted hundreds of godchildren during his electoral and propaganda campaigns in the provinces. On other levels, however, the HCP was not ready to compromise with the churches. First, it refused any compromise with regard to the exemption from expropriation of church land, especially that of the Catholic church, which had been one of the greatest landowners. Likewise the tolerance toward parish schools did not last long. The measures for the dissolution of the religious orders affected, with a few exceptions, the teaching orders as well. The secularization of education, which most democratic parties approved, was not long in coming. Finally, if the HCP curbed the atheistic and anticlerical zeal of its most radical followers, the same was not true for the "clerical reaction." Such a reaction undoubtedly existed. In the minds of certain prelates, the defense of the church was confounded with the defense of the politics of the past. This was true of Cardinal Mindszenty and other, less-known ecclesiastics. The hostile attitude of these clergymen, however, furnished the HCP an easy pretext for attacking all too assertive ecclesiastics and thus prepared the way for the police repression that was not long in coming down on them.

Returning to the analysis of the strategy and of the tactics of the HCP in the first years after the war, a conclusion is evident. The element of violence reappears indisputably and probably inevitably. Contrary to appearances, tactics and strategy actually do not overlap. If the HCP had not had designs other than those it proclaimed, it could have given up violence and waited peacefully for its "national" and reformist politics to produce their effect and win favor with the voters again. But the partial success or partial failure of the free elections radicalized it, leading it to take a harder line. This became more evident as relations among the wartime allies deteriorated. Thus violence recovered its place in HCP tactics, except for one difference from the past: the party now had the means for it. It had coercive means that were all the more formidable as they were based on the support of the Soviet Army. But it also had political means: the masses and the party organization. Certainly, the HCP did not succeed in becoming a class party, the party of the proletariat it so ardently wanted to be. It has remained after 1945 as before: an anomalous party without real social cohesion. But organization and discipline, the famous "party spirit," superseded the lack of social cohesion. The party, henceforth, no longer consisted of small groups that appealed to other small groups. It was a massive, dynamic, and disciplined political force, a force that mobilized the masses and succeeded in imposing its will on the majority of the population and on the other parties.

After this has been said, one is confronted with the eternal problem of the HCP's seizure of power in 1948, which put a brutal end to the tactics of the fronts, to the coalition, to national politics, and to everything else. The "salami tactics" led the Hungarian CP more gradually to it than was the case in Poland or in Czechoslovakia, but the result was the same. After the absorption of the SDP, the HCP had sole power.

Was this seen in advance, prepared and drafted from Moscow, as the partisans of the "blueprint theory" affirm? Or was the HCP in 1945 itself in the unknown, ready to play the game of the democratic fronts? Or did the favorable concurrence of circumstances itself begin the process of the seizure of power? The opinion of historians remains divided, and, for want of being able to consult the jealously guarded documents in the archives of the Kremlin, it is not possible to resolve the question. In the specific case of Hungary, there is nevertheless an element that makes the author of this study as well as other historians lean toward the second version. In 1948, namely, the leading team of the HCP seems itself to have been taken unawares by the turn of events. Proof for this is the self-criticism expressed by Mátyás Rákosi and, even more explicitly, by József Révai, about the conception of the "people's democracy." We have made a mistake, they declared in essence, by considering the new democracy as something durable and as a form of state and society fundamentally different from that of the Soviet Union. In fact, the people's democracy is nothing other than a "relatively peaceful passage" to socialism. Finally, the people's democracy, descended from the people's democratic revolution, is a "special form of the dictatorship of the proletariat"; were it not for the absence of the soviets, nothing would distinguish it from the one in the Soviet Union.

Are Rákosi and Révai trying to hoodwink the people—as

was the case in the manifestations of moderation, nationalism, and antisectarianism of the previous years? Nothing is
impossible, but then why did this "ideological rectification"
have to take the form of self-criticism? One rather has the
impression that the leaders of the HCP had retroactively to
shoulder the responsibility for a change that had occurred in
the politics of Stalin. The 1948 change was decisive, but its
beginning—at the Cominform conference in the fall of 1947—
was probably not as decisive as one thinks *a posteriori.* This
is especially so since the Yugoslav party, which was noted for
its revolutionary zeal, meanwhile had just been condemned
by Stalin, primarily because of its leftist excess. The Hungarian leaders consequently could believe that although they
were obligated to speed up the political and economic transformations, they had no reason whatever to make such
changes on the tactical level and even less reason to give up
the strategic "frontist" line.

The reinterpretation of the people's democracy by
Rákosi and Révai was followed by other restatements: for
example, the refutation of Lukács's theses about the new
democracy. These restatements were often rather tardy,
which further confirms the impression that the leading circles
were uncertain about the future of the people's democracies.
In short, many signs lead one to believe that directly after the
war and until around the end of 1947, the HCP came to expect
a long—perhaps a very long—period of "transition." Yet it
never gave up the "final goal" of someday reaching the communist society. But that is not the point. In assuming a
"transition" not of three but of thirty years, for example, the
politics of the fronts and of the new democracy could well
have been at the basis of the HCP's "strategy"; on the other
hand, the seizure of power—whether sudden as in Prague or
more progressive as in Budapest—brutally interrupted the anticipated course of events. The contrary hypothesis, of
course, is that the coup d'état was anticipated from the very
beginning and meticulously prepared long years in advance.

Events would seem to confirm this hypothesis. However, could there not be an intermediary explanation? To "wait and see," to be on the lookout and act according to circumstances—this is not exclusively an Anglo-Saxon attitude. Communists of all origins have practiced it more than once in their history. As one reads in the *History of the Hungarian Workers' Movement*:

> In the course of the development of the people's democracy, the dictatorship of the proletariat was established. However, the ideological clarification of the modified character of the political system has not taken place. . . . The leaders of the party have upheld their opinion . . . to attain socialism by way of the people's democracy without the dictatorship of the proletariat. In the end, the leaders of the people's democracies, after having consulted Stalin, found out at the end of 1948 that the people's democracy already fulfilled the function of the dictatorship of the proletariat in our countries.[19]

This text is very revealing: both in its language (our translation is very approximate) and in the information it contains. If it is exact, then it was entirely the *new instructions from Stalin* that compelled the leaders of the satellite communist parties to "proclaim" the dictatorship of the proletariat retroactively as well as to adapt reality to fiction as rapidly as possible.

In the end, the question arises whether the Hungarian communist leaders might have differed about the strategy of the frontist democracy. Without the shadow of a doubt, such differences had existed among the communists who emigrated to the Soviet Union. After 1935, the "antisectarians" —or those who were rapidly becoming such—prevailed. Therefore, with the help of the purges, a small group that was unconditionally obedient to the Kremlin emerged and checked any "leftist" inclination by getting rid of their rivals at the same stroke. This, among other factors, explains why so few Muscovites were placed in a position of command in Hungary after the war. Those who returned may have protested among one another, but they did not dare to proclaim convictions of "the 1919 style," much less criticize the official party line. Another category of "leftists," namely, the factionists of the interior such as Demény and his partisans were quickly eliminated—by the police. If the HCP hesitated perhaps a moment before making use of police methods against its democratic partners, it did so without scruples against its own black sheep. Under these conditions, what else could have given rise to this "sectarian danger" and this "nostalgia for 1919" with which Rákosi and his peers kept dinning the ears of the public; after all, most did not even know what these strange notions could possibly signify. According to an unpublished and remarkably well documented study by William O. McCagg, the phantom of sectarianism was brandished only in order to mask the "rightist" politics of Rákosi or—we would rather say—to give more credibility to frontist politics.[20]

If the politics and methods of the Hungarian CP present some special traits in regard to the other communist parties until 1948, this was not the case in the following period. On the other hand, since 1953, the ways of the HCP have again branched off from the normal path of the people's democracies. Foremost in the anti-Titoist crusade and in the sovietization of the country during the years when Stalinism predominated, the HCP effected a most spectacular turnabout in June 1953. As for its tactics, the "reform era" of 1953-1955 was until then an unprecedented variant of "enlightened communism" (according to the expression of François Fejtö). Certainly, the isolated and almost solitary moving spirit and promoter of the "June politics," Imre Nagy, attempted to introduce "frontist" elements into it by seeking especially the support of populist and nonparty writers as well as by trying to reinvigorate the front—which still existed on paper—but this does not constitute his true originality. His unique experiment was to humanize the system, as Dubček's group was to do twelve years later in Czechoslovakia. To redress wrongs, to release and rehabilitate the victims of police arbitrariness, to loosen the screws of economic constraint and other measures of this kind—this was only the material aspect. Even at that, because of the hostility of Rákosi and Gerö and of the apparatus in general, the changes were kept to a minimum. What Nagy wanted was to re-create—or rather really create—a climate of confidence and reestablish communication between the party and the people. The other original feature of his experiment was precisely the hostility on the part of the other communist leaders and of the apparatus. For the first time in the history of communism, a minuscule group, reduced practically to Nagy and his personal collaborators, attempted to reverse the engine in the face of a suspicious, even hostile, apparatus. In the later experiment of the "Prague Spring," the situation was more favorable because the party almost completely rallied to Dubček's line. In the case of Nagy and his friends, one cannot really speak of new tactics of the party but only of a group within the party. In this sense, the experiment of Hungary only reveals potential tactics, tactics that can prevail only under exceptional conditions. In the first place, it was necessary to have Moscow's support—even its initial encouragement—in order to attempt this experiment in humanization. Second, in order to pursue it, an appeal had to be made to the moral conscience, which had long been anaesthetized, of the communist elite. This was still another original aspect of the reform era of 1953-1955. It was only through a genuine crisis of conscience among the communists—a crisis that we shall discuss later—that the resistance of the bureaucratic apparatus could be at least neutralized, even shaken, for a certain period. There was too little time, however, to see the experiment through; it finally ran aground on the rock of this same bureaucracy, on the one hand, and on a temporary stiffening in Khrushchev's politics of de-Stalinization on the other.

Let us here pass over the turmoil of the revolution of 1956 as well as the first years of Kádár's regime, which, after the collapse of the previous regime, assumed control. After a difficult period of consolidation, the Kádár regime again presented original tactical traits, traits untried in the history of communism. It has often been argued that the Kádár regime picked up only the crumbs of the revolutionary program in order to ensure its own lines of communication and establish its own popularity. This is a tempting thesis. The idea that the gravediggers of revolutions become, owing to the dialectical nature of history, the executors of these very revolutions has long fascinated scholars. But this idea is only a half-truth, a half-truth based on the fact that ruptures are never total, that a certain continuity runs through the turmoil. In point of fact, the Kádár regime resumed the policies of the period before the revolution, namely, Imre Nagy's reform era and the agitated summer and fall of 1956, not the revolution itself. It reestablished a continuity shattered by the October events: the continuity of a prudent and moderated reformism. In this sense Kádár is, paradoxically, the heir of the prerevolutionary politics of Imre Nagy.

In many respects, his politics go even further than those of the June 1953 program. On the economic level, especially, there can be no comparison between the hasty improvisations of the reform era and the "new economic mechanism," which was put into place after several years of studies and which is based today on long experience. As for "socialist legality," the successes are also undeniable and even more extensive, if only because the present HCP has spent a great deal of time to make its police less arbitrary and its justice worthier of the name. One of the most spectacular successes has come in the most difficult field: agriculture. The HCP has been able, after a long and prudent wait followed by a violent attack against the peasantry, to be sure, to carry out an almost total collectivization without endangering production. On the contrary, Hungarian agriculture has become profitable, the cooperatives prosper or at the very least function well, their activity becomes diversified, and the rural standard of living rises constantly.

A complete inventory of the accomplishments would be as long as an inventory of the failures and weaknesses. But the balance is positive in the sense that the tactics of the regime have eventually overcome popular resistance and rallied public opinion. For its part, the Kádár regime enjoys a certain popularity, which allows it to maintain a serene political climate and to advance with circumspection down the path of enlightened reformism. What it lacks compared to the reform era as well as to the feverish summer of 1956, is the élan and the enthusiasm of great expectations. Hungarian public opinion does not expect wonders; it contents itself with its relative freedom and slow improvement and hopes above all that this may last. Kádár's popularity rests in fact on the fear of something worse.

The Crises of the HCP
since Its Accession to Power

It is difficult to define what a party crisis is. In a strict sense, the HCP has had only to overcome a single serious crisis, that of 1956, which again called into question if not its existence at least its authority, its program and ideology, its organizations and methods, and its leaders and cadres. The HCP was literally crushed on the night of October 23-24, 1956. We have already evoked the image of the officials of the apparatus pent up in the building at Akadémia Street, headquarters of the Central Committee. In that same house the (incomplete) Central Committee hastily convened in order to deliberate on the situation and the measures to take. Nothing shows its total impotence in the face of the insurrection that was raging on the streets more than the fact that the only measure it was capable of taking was to appeal to Imre Nagy and to some of his friends, who had hardly been reinstated in the party. One has rarely seen an ascent such as

Imre Nagy's. Expelled from the party in the wake of the resolutions that had condemned his "rightist" politics during the reform era of 1953-1955, he had just been readmitted to it as a simple member without title or rank. In spite of all this, within one night Nagy was co-opted into the Central Committee, elected a member of the Politburo, and charged with forming, with the assent of the head of state, a new government in order to confront the revolution.

According to certain opinions, which are entirely theoretical and formulated *a posteriori*, the party thereby committed an error. Instead of making an appeal to Imre Nagy, the party should have fought and crushed the "counterrevolution." That is indeed possible. But it did not fight and probably not only because of a momentary panic. Everything leads one to believe that the HCP very simply did not have the means to fight, even against the two thousand insurgents of the first hours. This exceptional phenomenon cannot be explained in terms of power relations. The barracks of the political police (AVH) held literally thousands of police armed to the teeth and faithful to the party, if only because their own existence was at stake. Likewise, thousands of militants, members of the apparatus, and other communists would have been ready to take up arms and defend the regime —it does not matter much whether it was for their own interest or for that of the cause. Finally, despite the demoralization of the army, the communist general could have formed at the very least a few officer units and thereby a force largely superior to that of the insurrection. Moreover, the Soviet tank units that the HCP and the government had called to the rescue had already begun action against the insurgents, who were armed with a few guns and Molotov cocktails.

The cause of the HCP's impotence was not of a material nature. Nor was it a political error or a poor analysis of the situation. It was a moral impotence. If the situation had been misjudged, the total demoralization of the party was at the root of the misjudgment. Not the insignificant weight of the insurrection, but the weight of the past prevented the party from facing the angry people. Likewise it was not one political quality of Imre Nagy or the absence of another that led the Central Committee to choose him; it was the fact that Nagy was the party's only link with the population.

In this sense, the crisis of the party at the crucial moment of October 1956 was part of an infinitely greater crisis. If the party found itself completely paralyzed at the decisive moment, if its powerful organization disintegrated all at once, if its combat forces were condemned to remain in their quarters, it is becaue a moral crisis had long been corroding it. In other words, the collapse of 1956 was the consequence of a series of crises, conflicts, and ailments, which had already manifested themselves with more or less acuteness throughout the preceding decade. Rajk's trial, followed by other fabricated trials against thousands of party militants, was the real starting point for it. The literary trials, especially the witch-hunt against Georg Lukács, were, to say the least, the symptoms of a profound uneasiness. Finally, the crisis of Rákosi's Stalinist regime also surfaced publicly between 1953 and 1956 after the disclosure of the police atrocities and abuses of justice that had occurred in the Stalinists' struggle against Imre Nagy and his fellow reformers.

Of all that generated the acute and devastating crisis of 1956, it was the police system that weighed most heavily. It was precisely the police system that demoralized the party. At the same time, it was one of the determining factors of the collective behavior of the communists, a question that shall be discussed in our last chapter.

The political police—later AVO and after that AVH (State Security Authority)—was originally limited to the pursuit of activities against the security of the new democratic state order as well as to investigations and interrogations against the fascist war criminals. Its headquarters were in a large building on Andrássy Street (later renamed Stalin

Street), in the former headquarters of the Arrow Cross party, the nazi-fascist party that had spread panic during its reign from October 15, 1944, until the liberation of Budapest from German occupation. As the HCP struggled, first against the conservative parties and afterward against its reluctant democratic partners, the political police became an extremely powerful political instrument in its hands. It had very quickly disposed of any element the party thought unsafe, especially the officers whom other parties of the coalition had placed in it. Deputy chief, then chief, of the AVO, Gábor Péter was actually subordinate only to the "big four" of the HCP and very often received his orders directly from Mátyás Rákosi. Among the ministers of the interior, the hierarchical bosses of the political police, only László Rajk, who held this post between 1946 and 1948, had the right to control the police. Péter, this former militant, a tailor by profession, weak and unintelligent, was entirely devoted to Rákosi, who in turn made him his principal liege and a most feared individual. Péter for his part surrounded himself with a general staff and an officer corps in his image. Many of them came from a lower-middle-class Jewish background, which only added another element to the already complex Jewish problem.

As long as the AVO (and AVH) was active outside the ranks of the party, the rumors that circulated about its violence and tortures did not excessively trouble the good communist conscience. Most militants simply refused to hear about them or explained away the "irregularities" with reference to the difficult struggle first against the fascist reaction, then against the clerical reaction and various others after that: politicians of the moderate parties, social democrats, kulaks. Even during the thaw, Imre Nagy was the first and practically the only highly placed communist who admitted and deplored the "illegalities" committed against non-communist elements.

The deep uneasiness within the HCP started with the Rajk affair. The arrest, trial, and execution of the former minister of the interior and his unfortunate companions were, on the other hand, a terrible shock, since it could only be assuaged and faced after Stalin's death and even then with painful slowness. For five years, not only the population but also the party lived in an atmosphere of fear constantly maintained by new arrests. Hundreds of communists, the best known and the unknown, fell victim to this permanent purge, among others Tibor Szönyi, András Szalai, György Pálffy, János Kádár, Gyula Kállai, Sándor Haraszti, Géza Losonczy, Ferenc Donáth, László Gács, László Sólyom, Gyula Oszkó, and Béla Szász.

The most disturbing was the antimony between the alleged crimes—spying, treason, conspiracy against the party—and the stature of the alleged criminals. Just as in the Stalinist trials, the accused (or the missing) came from the party elite. They were former militants, victims of repression during the Horthy regime, volunteers in the International Brigades in Spain, antifascist resistance fighters, members of the Central Committee, ministers, generals, and prestigious intellectuals. Many were of Jewish origin. All without exception belonged to the "interior" party without Muscovite antecedent. There were many veterans from the Spanish war and members of the armed forces. The trend was clear. The aim was to eliminate what remained of the illegal HCP, to tear up, so to speak, its inadequate "letters of nobility." The frequent reference to the complicity of the condemned persons with Tito strengthened this impression, which was at the same time emphasized by the already disturbing fact of the excommunication of the Yugoslav communists, formerly the pride of the international communist movement. Who was not suspect, who was safe from arrests and prisons if all these people could fall from the pedestal? Regardless of whether they agreed that the accusations had solid grounds, all communists henceforth experienced a permanent feeling of uneasiness and insecurity.

This complex feeling of uneasiness and culpability appeared in Hungary from 1953-1956, when the prisons and the concentration camps opened their gates and when among tens of thousands of released survivors, hundreds, perhaps thousands, of communists returned home.

The diabolical "mechanism" of the purges is too well known and the Hungarian example too like the others for us to describe them. The only point in which the Hungarian case is somewhat different from the others was that the rehabilitations started earlier in Hungary than elsewhere—1954—and that they provoked a real storm. At first, as the accounts of the survivors revealed all the horror, if not the details of the atrocities, of police procedure and justice, there was a storm of indignation and shame.[21] Unlike other communist countries, Hungary at once raised the question of the responsibility of the party and its leaders. The elimination of a few scapegoats appeased neither the conscience nor the remorse these "affairs" had stirred up. Thus in a second period, in particular after Khrushchev's disclosures at the Twentieth Congress of the Soviet Communist party, Hungary became the scene of a real escalation of political and moral claims: the total rehabilitation of László Rajk and his companions, the review of all trials, and the punishment of those responsible, including Mátyás Rákosi himself. There was an even harder blow for the leaders: the dispute, until then limited to the intellectuals of the party, spread to other communist circles, such as the army and even the periphery of the apparatus. The "unconditionals," those linked to the leading group for various reasons, were on the defensive, lost their former boldness, and became uneasy and disoriented.

We have deliberately omitted other aspects of the crisis: bad economic management, the complete alienation of the peasantry, and the more and more burdensome Soviet influence. The importance of these factors is evident, and their repercussions on the party, the only one responsible for the catastrophic situation in the country, are equally evident. We have preferred, however, to put the accent on the moral degradation, which from 1949 grew worse and worse and eventually caused the disarray of the communists as well as the discomposure of the party at the moment when the angry people, until then the silent actor, appeared on the scene.

For the Kádár regime, which was established as a result of the intervention of the Soviet tanks, it was not easy to reverse the current. It was confronted with a long, firm, and relentless passive resistance that paralyzed life in Hungary for several months. Therefore, police repression resumed worse than ever, this time against opponents such as the leaders of the workers' councils and against those who were allegedly responsible for the October 1956 events. Accused of being counterrevolutionaries, thousands of persons again passed through the same prisons that János Kádár and Gyula Kállai had known. In June 1958, a horrified public learned of the execution of Imre Nagy and three of his codefendants, who until recently had still been companions of the party leader, János Kádár. According to certain unofficial sources, Kádár would not have done something so irreversible had he not been forced to by the Soviet leaders, who were themselves pushed . . . by the Chinese. Everything is possible. Still, the fact remains that other executions took place after trials that were conducted behind closed doors, unnoticed and without publicity. Other trials had a less fatal outcome. Among others, such world-famous writers as Tibor Déry and Julius Háy and many others 'were brought to trial and given heavy sentences. Only in 1962—owing to pardons or the amnesty— did most of the workers, young people, officers, and intellectuals sentenced for their participation in the events of 1956 recover their freedom.

Since then, political trials have become rare, and police pressure has progressively weakened. Has the Kádár regime solved the problem of the police system? Nothing is less certain, in spite of the undeniable efforts of the new leaders and Kádár in person to do so. Lately, attention has again been called to police interventions with regard to certain intellectuals, writers, and sociologists. One of them was arraigned in court and acquitted. It is consequently not the seriousness of the new facts that can compel prudence as to whether a Hungarian communism can assume a human face and banish police methods. Nor is it the attitude of Kádár and his close collaborators. Their sincere intention is probably not to fall back into what is euphemistically called "the errors of the past." But the political infrastructure of the regime has not really changed, which always makes it possible to turn backward. Moreover, the present leaders do not really control their own political police. The political police is invariably subordinate to the Soviet police services, especially through the Russian "advisors" assigned to the Hungarian leaders. Kádár could probably have done away with this system in Khrushchev's time, but he did not feel it was then necessary. Later he could not get rid of it, even though he might have wanted to.

Nevertheless, Hungary today as well as the party members enjoy a freedom and a climate of security that are only very relative in comparison to the Western democracies, but that make life much easier than in Rákosi's Hungary or in the other communist countries.

4. Foreign Relations

Before Tito's excommunication by the Cominform, the HCP had maintained privileged relations with Yugoslavia, which did not prevent the HCP from taking the opposite attitude when the insults of the communist parties came down on Yugoslavia. "As a matter of fact," the attorney general, Alapy, declared in the Rajk trial, "it is Tito and his accomplices who are sitting on the defendants' bench."[1] When the circumstances changed, Marshal Tito did not fail to pay Rákosi and his accomplices back in their own coin. After the spectacular reconciliation between Khrushchev and Tito, the latter demanded from the Hungarian CP a whole series of measures to make amends for the wrong that the particularly violent anti-Titoist campaign of the Hungarians had caused him. Only the humble self-criticism of the latter led him to agree, much against his will, to reestablish contact with the implicated leaders and, in October 1956, to let a Hungarian delegation led by Ernö Gerö come to Belgrade. For these reasons but also simply because Yugoslavia had for some time recovered its place as a privileged ally of the Kremlin, the "Yugoslav factor" played an important role in the ferment of 1956. Certainly, the angry people who eventually descended into the streets of Budapest cared little about Tito. On the other hand, the opposition within the party did not fail to refer to the Yugoslav experiment, emphasizing that imitation

of the Soviet Union was not the rule and that by reconciling
with Belgrade, Moscow had acknowledged the existence of
"special paths" toward socialism. Moreover, certain members
of the opposition had been so audacious as to maintain relations with Yugoslav communists, who, for their own part,
encouraged the opposition movement. It seems that in the
summer and fall of 1956, the possibility of Imre Nagy's
return to power was not displeasing to the Belgrade leaders,
especially Kardelj, who, according to certain information,
wanted to keep more distance toward Moscow than Tito and
because of that wished to stimulate tendencies toward
autonomy within the Hungarian CP. On November 4, 1956,
as is known, the Yugoslav embassy in Budapest offered
asylum to Imre Nagy and his friends.

Nevertheless, the events of October and November created reservations in Belgrade. The revolution was not the
same thing as the reformism and the "national path" of the
Yugoslav kind. In Tito's eyes, Imre Nagy, whom events had
passed by even before he was ousted by Russian tanks, was
no longer of great value as a potential ally. On the eve of the
Soviet intervention of November 4, Tito is even said to have
given his assent to Khrushchev, who had come expressly to
see him in order to have this decision endorsed.[2]

In these conditions, the welcome for Imre Nagy and his
group at the Yugoslav embassy in Budapest had no relation
to the events and was probably the result of a previous decision. It may have been sheer duplicity. If Belgrade had let a
Hungarian countergovernment form in Yugoslavia, it would
have been a very risky move in this period of extreme
tension, when the Soviet Army deployed considerable forces
near the Yugoslav borders.

Whatever their intentions, the Yugoslav leaders quickly
abandoned Nagy's group. After a few days of negotiations,
the Hungarians who had sought refuge at the embassy were
handed over to the Soviets and deported, as already indicated, to Rumania. Certainly, the Yugoslav authorities pro-

tested against this, because, according to the agreement concluded with the Kádár government, Nagy and his friends had been given a safe-conduct and should have been able to return to their homes. The aftereffects of this epilogue were quickly eliminated, however, and since then Hungarian-Yugoslav relations, while experiencing ups and downs, have become normalized.

Various works often mention the traditional Polish-Hungarian friendship. But, it must be admitted, this tradition has amounted to very little after 1945. However, at the crucial moment of the 1956 events, the "Polish factor" took on a rather extraordinary importance, proving how durable collective mental structures can be. As is well known, the events in Warsaw that brought Gomułka to power started a row in Budapest: the revolution began as a demonstration of solidarity with the fraternal Polish people. On the other hand, Polish public opinion, even Gomułka's CP, continued to lend support to the Hungarian cause even when Tito had already recanted and when European opinion had turned to other preoccupations, especially the Suez affair.

The relations of the HCP with the other people's democracies have never departed from routine. The only exception to this rule was the crisis of Prague in 1968. Kádár's attitude has had the consequence that since then, the hard-line communist parties of the Soviet camp, that is, those of Czechoslovakia and East Germany, have looked unfavorably upon the liberal experiment developing in Hungary. Above all the German CP was probably implicated in the pressures that the "communist community" has exerted on the leadership of the Hungarian CP, which is considered rather too liberal. Too little information has leaked out to know enough about it, but the affair is probably far from over and Kádár and his already decimated team will probably have to face other attempts to "bring them into line."

The HCP's attitude toward the Western countries has always been and remains extremely cautious. Hitler's last satellite, Hungary, was in an awkward position after the war; as in 1920, moreover, it was treated without consideration by the Allies. During the Rákosi era, the foreign policy of the HCP consisted in "supporting" the antiimperialistic campaign of the Soviet Union. Détente was not to bring great innovations. It only liquidated certain minor affairs in litigation and allowed the normalization of diplomatic relations with some Western countries. On this level, the behavior of Kádár's HCP has hardly changed anything. Although eager, for obvious economic reasons, to draw nearer to the Federal Republic of Germany, Hungary was one of the last countries to resume diplomatic relations with it.

Prudence and moderation also prevail with regard to the great Western communist parties. The HCP takes care not to get involved in the polemics that often enough divide the fraternal parties, especially the Italian and French. The party press, though aligning itself with Moscow's position, avoids as best it can such controversial issues as China or Cuba, which today have been toned down.

In a general way, today as before, the Hungarian CP does not behave with much éclat toward foreign countries. For one reason or another and despite the explosion of 1956, Hungary has proved to be the most obedient satellite of the Soviet Union. Shortly after the war, it made heavy sacrifices in order to satisfy Moscow's most excessive economic demands. It was the first to comply to the letter with the sovietization of its economy, its politics, and its culture. The Hungarian CP hurled the rudest insults against Tito (when it was instructed to do so) and against the United States during the Cold War. If the tone has changed since 1957, the content has not. Moscow can always count on the "support" of the Hungarian CP.

Budapest's practically unconditional alignment with Moscow has made it difficult for the audacious experiments to make its regime viable to be understood. It is difficult to judge whether that is good or bad. But only at this price can the HCP pursue—until further notice—its politics of prudent reforms in the rather hostile, or at the very least suspicious, milieu of the communist bloc that surrounds it.

Besides, circumstances are responsible for the fact that the Hungarian party will never be able to loosen the vise of the Soviet party's tutelage, not even to the modest extent that the Rumanians and the Poles have. The reasons for this are diverse, although in essence it is only a question of variations on two themes: the internal weakness of the HCP, which always made it dependent on Moscow, and Hungary's vulnerability as a small country without resources.

The history and the organization of the HCP have shown the various aspects of this dependence, as has been mentioned several times. We shall refer here only to certain themes.

Theoretically, the party of the first and only Republic of the Councils in Central Europe was well placed to resume its role of avant-garde after World War II. In principle at least, it also had the necessary cadres because of the number and the quality of its Muscovite emigration. If such was not the case, it was primarily because these same cadres were progressively liquidated. Certainly, time also accomplished its work. The communist militants of Béla Kun's commune had been relatively young, but twenty-five years later their average age was between fifty and sixty years. Rákosi was fifty-three years old in 1945, Gerö and Révai forty-seven, Imre Nagy forty-nine, Georg Lukács sixty. Others died a natural death (Jenö Landler), still others perished on the Spanish front (Máté Zalka [General Lukács]) or in active service in Hungary or even during the war. Nevertheless, neither the war nor Horthy's prisons and tribunals created such a holocaust as Stalin's purges. There is now not enough information to advance precise and comparable figures. However, it is enough to examine the available information in order to get some idea about it. The work of Endre Sik and the Historical Dictionary of the Workers' Movement indicate that about

seventy to eighty persons were arrested during the purges, of
whom fifty-three were executed or disappeared in concentration camps.[3] It must be noted that Sik speaks only of his
personal acquaintances and that the dictionary obviously
mentions only the more important militants. Thus, there are
notable omissions: also arrested were Georg Lukács, László
Rudas, Ernö Czóbel, Ernö Bettelheim, Béla Szántó, Zoltán
and Ferenc Bíró (Rákosi's brothers), to mention only a few
well-known cases. Another indication of the extent of the
purges is the fate of the ten people's commissars—that is,
ministers of the government of the Councils of Hungary—
indicted in 1920 in Budapest. The judges of Budapest handed
down four convictions of capital punishment and six of life
imprisonment. Later, the ten former commissars arrived in
Moscow through the prisoner exchange, which we have
already mentioned. One of them died in his bed in 1927,
three were soon able to leave Russia and establish themselves
in Western Europe, one returned to Hungary as a retired
person in 1945, and the other five perished in the purges.
Moreover, most of the seventy to eighty cases (see the two
abovementioned sources) are said to have been commissars or
deputy commissars, general officers, or members of the Central Committee of the HCP, either during the Republic of the
Councils or during the underground years. The proportion of
leaders purged is thus extremely high: fifty-three executions
and disappearances in seventy to eighty arrests. That is, there
were only about twenty survivors among the notables listed
in a biographical dictionary of the HCP. In addition, the
survivors have often not been allowed to go back to Hungary
or received permission to do so only several years after the
liberation. All things considered, our calculations with
respect to the purges confirm our previous statement: the
HCP in 1945 profited very little from the experience of the
militants who returned from Moscow; very few of them were
placed in political positions of command.

In short, the group of Muscovites established in power in

1945 was recruited from the second rank of the émigrés: Rákosi, Gerö, Révai, Farkas, Imre Nagy, József Gábor, Géza Révész, Sándor Nógrádi, and perhaps about ten others. They had various qualifications. None of them had been imprisoned in Russia. On the contrary, since 1940-1941, the Soviet authorities had picked them to take over from the former leaders. Strengthened by this support, the group was charged during the war with directing the broadcasts of radio Kossuth, the publications destined for the Hungarian prisoners of war, as well as the antifascist schools for the formation of future cadres. They were assisted by a group of intellectuals, either survivors of the purges or escapees from Stalin's prisons: e.g., the writers and journalists Illés, Gábor, Gergely, and Háy as well as Mmes. Kenyeres, Lányi, Fazekas, and others.

A conclusion is evident: in 1945 a group of subordinate communist officials assumed the leadership of the HCP, officials who had neither the international reputation of Kun and Landler, nor the experience of Szántó and Vági, nor the ideological fame of a Lukács, nor the artistic reputation of a Béla Uitz. They could not but comply to the letter with the orders of the Kremlin; they had to be overzealous in order to prove their absolute loyalty. Stalin's idea to make Rákosi, Gerö, Révai, and Farkas (all four were from families of small Jewish merchants or clerks) his foremost agents could only increase their total dependence on the good graces of Moscow. Stalin was probably well aware of the fact that Hungarian public opinion would never accept this group.

In addition, a complex system of Soviet agents was established in the first hours of the Soviet occupation. These were not only the Soviet occupation authorities, to whom the armistice convention gave political, military, economic, police, and censorship powers, a fact without precedent in European history. Simultaneously, other Soviet agencies were established to control domains as varied as the operation of the numerous so-called mixed economic societies (e.g.,

shipping, civil aviation, mining of various minerals) or the distribution of films. It is not necessary to dwell on the decisive
role that Soviet advisors played in the army, the police, and
the ministries. As far as political direction at the upper
echelons is concerned, information is fragmentary. As long as
Marshal Voroshilov was head of the Allied Control Commission, the Kremlin had an authoritative representative on the
spot. Did the Soviet embassy entirely resume the role played
by the Marshal and his collaborators? Once more, information is sketchy and questionable. It is known that in the years
1953-1956 highly placed Soviet diplomats and in particular
Yuri Andropov, future head of the MGB, interfered directly
in party affairs. It is less certain that the embassy played
quite so direct a role in other periods. In Rákosi's time, the
instructions came from the Kremlin, often from Stalin himself. At what moments, how often, why, and in what circumstances did the leaders of the Hungarian CP receive instructions? Once more, the historian is reduced to risky hypotheses
—except for the meetings of 1953-1955, of which Imre
Nagy's memoirs give rather detailed accounts. The latter,
with the writings of Djilas and some Italian communists, are
the only authentic sources that permit us to imagine the tone
and the climate of the conversations between the Soviet comrades on one side and those of the people's democracies on
the other. These sources are more than mere fragments of
information; they confirm that the Soviets treated Rákosi
and consorts as subordinates who had only to receive orders—
or even as servants if the aggressive and arrogant tone of the
criticism aimed at them is any indication.

Relations between Budapest and Moscow have probably
changed little since that time. The tone and climate may have
changed. But the content has not. The Hungarian CP is still
militarily and politically dependent on the Kremlin as well as
on the various control channels the Soviets have—from
bilateral relations to political instruments such as the Warsaw
Pact as well as the presence of the advisors and the Soviet

Army on Hungarian territory. In short, the sovereignty of the HCP is as fictitious with regard to the essentials as is that of the country itself. On the other hand, inside this iron collar, the HCP has relative freedom of movement, which probably goes together with a more polite tone and expression in Soviet-Hungarian relations. For reasons of international prestige, in order to look after its image, and because of changes inside the Soviet CP itself, the leaders of the Kremlin would not easily resort to force again against one or the other of their rebellious satellites. Thus they must listen to them, to discuss, to bargain if necessary. This happens more and more often, especially on the level of economic relations, as several Comecan meetings and especially the case of Rumania prove. Without going that far, the leaders of the Hungarian CP, too, are more determined than ever to refuse to sacrifice the interests of their own country for the benefit of the mother country of international communism. All this is part of an evolution that characterizes all communist parties in power, but especially that of Hungary. Established with the help of Soviet power and dependent on it on more than one level, the HCP has become, through the natural process of interaction and interdependency with the population, a responsible government.

5. Conclusion

The determining factors of the HCP's behavior are inscribed in its structure and in its history. At the same time, another general remark must be made, namely, that the changes that have occurred through its rise to power mark its behavior deeper than its pre-1945 heritage. These concluding remarks will not recall what was said earlier about its character as a "counter-police" toward the authorities and as a small group organized, but deprived of social coherence, in prewar society. Even if these prewar character traits were evident for some time yet (as was the case with the spirit of conspiracy, suspicion, and sectarianism, which were certainly combated on the political level, but remained virulent on an individual level) other traits soon became dominant. This is the same for the barely perceptible heritage of 1919. The HCP's behavior in 1948 is that of the winner, a winner full of confidence. It is convinced, owing to the ideology of which it is the trustee, that historical truth and justice are on its side. At the same time, it is a winner uncertain of its foundations and all the more prone to violence, arrogance, and intolerance. But these traits are no longer those of an insignificant small group. They are those of an organization that has practically unlimited means of coercion at its disposal.

There was perhaps a transition period during which the traditions, structures, and mentalities of the small group of yesteryear and those of the mass party with one million members came into contact or overlapped. But by 1950 not much was left of the past save the inclination to violence and the climate of suspicion—maintained and generalized by the Soviet graft the "Muscovite" leaders brought with them. As for the former leaders from within Hungary, they remained few in number in the command posts of the "new" party, the party in power. If we could identify only about twenty survivors of Stalin's prisons and some scores of others spared by the purges and returned to Hungary, then the list of the "old-timers" of the interior would not give considerably different results. The sources we consulted yielded 119 persons who had held, at one time or another before the end of the war, leading positions: members of the Central Committee or of the provisional committees. Eighteen of them reappear in the central committees after 1945 (but before 1956); of these, nine are also members of the Politburo. As for the 101 others, dead, disappeared, or discarded from the leadership of the party, there are traces of only several. Seven were executed in Hungary before 1945, two were killed in Nazi prisons, and at least twenty were executed or died in Stalin's prisons, that is, twenty-nine altogether.[1] About the seventy-two other former leaders who have not resumed their positions after 1945, we have gathered many different pieces of information. Some died, others left the country, some left the party and the workers' movement, and still others remained there in more modest functions. Whatever the reason was, however, their fate shows a profound break of continuity between the old party and the new one, at least in the upper echelon. The purges and the liquidations of the Rákosi era further widened this difference. Between 1945 and 1953, at least seven former members of previous central committees were imprisoned. One of them was executed (Rajk). Owing to successive purges, only nine remained in the Central Committee formed after the events of 1956. Their number increased, on the other hand, in the 1960s; the

HCP rescued from oblivion some "old-timers" of the underground period.

All these figures call for comments for the sake of precision. They may well give the false impression that there existed two groups—one "interior," the other "Muscovite"—entirely separate from each other. In fact, the two groups overlapped. Obviously, the 119 members of the various central committees and provisional committees include many Muscovite émigrés and the militants of the interior. Likewise, among the eighteen former leaders on the list of the central committees formed after 1945, there are also a certain number of Muscovites, e.g., Gerö, Rákosi, and Révai; on the other hand, the eighteen do not include Imre Nagy, Mihály Farkas, Zoltán Vas, István Kossa, and some others for the simple reason that they were not previously members of the Central Committee. Let us finally point out that it is impossible to guarantee that the number of those executed and imprisoned is exact. However, since we have taken the basic facts from official or authorized publications, the difference between reality and the figures thus obtained could not be very great. At the very least, these figures convey an order of magnitude, which allows the reader to form an idea of the fate of 111 persons as well as of the "change and continuity" in the leadership of the HCP.

From counter-police having become police, the HCP, as we have pointed out, was deeply marked by the arrests and trials on which, in the absence of sufficiently large social foundations, its power is based. Furthermore, one must not only consider the agents of the political police (AVH), its investigations and its arbitrary interrogations, and its methods of physical and moral torture, but also the confusion of the political and police functions. On the one hand, the party controls its political police, points out and hands over the accused to it, and sees to it that the police cannot become a parallel power. The limits of this control are, however, clearly defined by the great control the Soviets exert in this domain. Therefore the party has as much a hold on the AVH as the AVH has on the party. The preservation of this delicate and fragile equilibrium is a variable factor, certainly, at the mercy of circumstances, but it remains at all times one of the principal preoccupations of the HCP.

On the other hand, to the extent that the political police acts as the organ of coercion of the party, the latter inspires a feeling of terror in the population—even if, as now, this terror exerts itself only in limited cases. Potentially, it always exists and thus maintains the rift between the party and society.

In a remarkable historical and sociological study, Annie Kriegel has defined the French Communist party especially as a "counter-society."[2] This definition is based, certainly, on data specific to the French situation; nevertheless, it also retains its value for the study of a communist party in power, such as the Hungarian party. The fact that the CP exerts power without having received a mandate from the people only makes it more of a counter-society. This situation obliges the party to draw its legitimacy from sources outside society, especially from ideology and history, more precisely from a certain interpretation of history. In this sense it has remained Marxist. Since History—with a capital *H*—"works" at its cause and will not fail to justify its final objective, that is, the affluent and classless communist society, the party gives itself the historic mission of reaching this objective. The theme is too well known for us to dwell on it. The essential point is to recall the fundamental duality in the operation of the HCP: it draws its legitimacy from the final goal, yet it has to rely upon the various means of control it has vis-à-vis society.

Obviously, the governmental system that is derived from it is precarious. The CP hardly has any alternative other than to keep this power in spite of all difficulties. Otherwise it could only abdicate or even, no doubt, transform itself into a social democratic party ready to share power or play the role of a progressive force or both. This change may be possible and valuable in countries such as France or Italy, but it is definitely inapplicable in a people's democracy such as Hungary. There, in the present state of affairs, the alternative is power at any price or voluntary or forced abdication.

However, it is not easy, nor perhaps possible in the long run, to base power on an abstract legitimacy. Therefore the CP attempts to found its legitimacy on other, complementary sources: economic, social, and cultural. As for constitutional legitimacy—through elections—the nature of these elections is only too well known. On the other levels mentioned— economic, social, and cultural—the question is to achieve the predominance of the working class as well as equality of opportunity for social mobility, democratization of knowledge, and, finally, affluence. There are so many substitutes because these measures neither in theory nor in practice necessitate a dictatorship of the proletariat, much less the monolithic power of a single party. If the CP's indisputable successes in these domains appear in its balance sheet as so much evidence of its management, their true function is to diminish the difference between the "counter-society in power" and the real society. By acting in this way, the CP recognizes that it cannot rule with bayonets, and, that on the other hand, it conforms to the nature of things that have made it the manager of society. For all that, no new source of legitimacy is created, no more than the rift is covered; but by acting as manager, the CP assumes a responsibility, a responsibility that determines its behavior as much as its role of "historical agent of the revolution" does—and even more. The old adage applies also to the CP: happy parties have no history. The Hungarian CP has, of course, a history. Kádár's CP attempts to do without it—which is why it strives to narrow to a minimum the rift that separates it from society and to reduce as much as possible its own character as counter-society. The *History of the Revolutionary Workers' Movement of Hungary* quotes a hitherto unpublished speech that Mátyás Rákosi gave before the Central Committee in 1949, in which he declared especially that "the comrades who believe that the Popular Front is a lasting phenomenon . . . are mistaken."[3] Simultaneously, the HCP launched the slogan, "He who is not with us, is against us." The present HCP, certainly, has not brought about a return to the Popular Front on the level of government and political power; nevertheless, it has reversed the slogan: now, "He who is not against us, is with us." Nothing could better illustrate the concern of János Kádár's party to become above all a good administrator, to manage affairs if not *uti pater familias* but in any case as a good merchant should.

This also accounts for the effort that characterizes the party and to which it grants priority, namely, to carry out the "new economic mechanism." In fact, the HCP's economic policy has always been a corollary of its general policy and, because of that, an indication, a kind of barometer of its behavior. The forced industrialization of 1950-1953 reflected the three major motivations of the HCP: the imitation of the Soviet model, a conception of development based on heavy industry and autarky, finally an offensive attitude in the eventuality of a war. For its part, however, the Kádár regime cares very little about the strategic objectives of yesteryear. It first attempted to improve the standard of living in order to gain time and to regain favor with public opinion. In its second period, which began with the economic reforms of the "new mechanism," it essentially aimed at establishing viable production and price structures and mechanisms. It is at this level that economic policy rejoins and overlaps with the good managerial behavior that the HCP seeks nowadays. It is consequently a "productivist" behavior, as one would say in current jargon. Certainly, the HCP has not transformed itself to the point of attempting to build its existence on other values. Like its brother parties, above all that of the Soviet Union, it little by little offers its citizens refrigerators, television sets, and cars. In short, it is a consumer society without capitalists. But unlike the others, it tries to reach this rapidly and without unnecessary sufferings and sacrifices.

The same concern can be felt in all the other domains of public life. The manager wants to form—through its successes —a technocracy that will earn the people's respect. But will it succeed in breaking up the resistance that its own structures offer? That is the question, that and the resistance of the international milieu, namely, that of the other communist capitals, which observe the Hungarian experiment with suspicion and hostility.

In other words, has the Hungarian CP ceased to be a counter-society? Has its own structure ceased to be an obstacle to the transformations for which it has itself taken the initiative? It is tempting to say that history will provide the answer. But it is possible that history will never answer this question, which touches on the very foundations of existing communist societies. The historical interest of the Hungarian experiment consists in the fact that Kádár's CP has pushed it, so it seems, to its extreme limits. But this apparatus, which wants—probably sincerely—to be a worthy manager, remains at the same time a "new class," a new establishment, a counter-police-become-police, a hierarchy of samurai with an honor code and a mode of behavior peculiar to its social and political status. But this status is based, it must be added, on the unshared power that it has not through the mandate of the people or that of the working class, but through the force and coercion at its disposal. In the last analysis, it does not matter much *how* it uses them. It has them. And it cannot give them up without compromising its raison d'être: power. That is the major obstacle to the abolition of the HCP as counter-society. This is a banal and disappointing conclusion, no doubt. But one can more easily imagine the HCP as defender of the national interests (which it makes its own toward other countries, even toward the Kremlin) than as a group that would allow its position and power again to be called into question. It seems condemned to be tossed eternally between the two waves that carry it: the responsibility of the governor toward the governed, on the one hand, and, on the other, the reality of the power of the privileged class that it is.

As a result of the organizational reforms and transformations, the HCP is beginning to emerge from the drowsiness of the past. There are signs that it now has more active contacts with the surrounding world. János Kádár, who had traveled only exceptionally in the Western world, went to Vienna in 1976 in order to meet Chancellor Kreiski and to Rome in 1977, where he was granted a remarkable audience by Pope Paul VI. On the other hand, not only businessmen but also more and more politicians, such as François Mitterand and Senator George McGovern, are visiting Hungary. The country and János Kádár himself enjoy favorable press comments in the Western world, where newspapers describe Hungary as the most liberal and most open-minded of all the communist countries. The Hungarian émigrés, not unmindful of the progress that has been made, are more moderate than the émigrés from other communist countries. They visit Hungary. Of the 200,000 Hungarian refugees from 1956, few have not yet spent their holidays in Budapest and at Lake Balaton.

Do these symptoms, which one could multiply, indicate that Kádár's Hungary, already more relaxed internally than the other communist countries, will also become more flexible in its international relationships? Some people call Hungary the future "bridge" between the communist and the Western world.

It is always precarious to make forecasts in political matters. It is even more so in the case of Hungary, since its political development depends on international factors, above all, on Moscow. Of the various external factors, there is one that could directly affect the international orientation of the HCP: Eurocommunism.

In 1956, when Togliatti and Tito developed the theses of the "polycentrism" of international communism (i.e., they questioned whether the Soviet Union would be the unique center and pattern of communism), the experiment made by Imre Nagy's first government in Hungary from 1953 to 1955 was very positively considered by the nonorthodox communists. Later on, the Italian, the French, the Chinese, and other communist parties condemned the Hungarian revolution of 1956 and its leader, Imre Nagy. They even approved, if only through their silence, the execution of Imre Nagy in June 1958. Nevertheless, Imre Nagy's memory remains alive among the communists of the so-called European tendency. To them, this affair has still not been settled and might again flare up. Was not Imre Nagy, well before Dubček, the first to speak about "communism which doesn't forget man"? Was he not the first "Eurocommunist," at a time when the Italians followed the Moscow line and the French were more Stalinist than Stalin himself? In 1976, on the twentieth anniversary of the Hungarian Revolution, some leaders of the Italian Communist party, if not Berlinguer himself, began to refine their judgment about the events of Budapest. This revision of judgment follows its course among the Eurocommunists and even on a larger scale. In its issue of September 1977, the historical review of the Rumanian Communist party, for example, describes the events that took place in 1956 in Hungary not as a counterrevolution, but as a righteous popular uprising. At the same time, many Eurocommunists believe that the success of Kádár's regime can be explained to a certain extent by the fact that the present leaders of the HCP have drawn reasonable conclusions from 1956, i.e., they have met several of the people's demands, especially with regard to the economy and human rights.

The communism of Hungary seems to be a model or, at least, a form of communism that is more acceptable to Western democratic traditions. This fact is significant, in spite of the small size of the country, and particularly so since 1975-1976, the years during which the Soviet Union's prestige among the Western communists and, generally speaking, the Left, fell to pieces. Since the death of Mao, Chinese communism has also lost the somewhat mythical prestige it enjoyed among certain factions of the Left. As for East Germany, its economic performances do not help us to forget its Prussian and Stalinist character. The communism of the most Westernized country in Central Europe, Czechoslovakia, has lost credit as a consequence of the uninterrupted repressions since 1968. Poland faces a long-lasting economic crisis and a discontented populace. Rumania has remained Stalinist, in spite of its relatively autonomous foreign policy. Under the circumstances, the relatively free and prosperous Hungary of Kádár has become an example, the only example Eurocommunism can offer. It is doubtlessly a "mini-model," but it is a model all the same. This explains the interest with which Western communists follow the Hungarian experiment.

Obviously, the Hungarian communist regime cannot remain indifferent to the favorable repercussions of its own experiments. This is not only a matter of prestige; a better reputation also has certain advantages—one has more confidence in a prosperous country with a tolerable political climate than in an impoverished police state. The foreign tourist has also become more confident, as shown by the considerable growth of tourism. In the final analysis, this confidence represents a political asset with its unpredicable consequences, even if it is for the time being but a modest hope.

The almost unique situation of the Hungarian communist regime is manifested by careful, but significant, moves. Beyond the prudent overtures toward Austria, Germany, and the United States (in particular since the election of President Carter), the HCP in power endeavors to enhance its Western image—the image of a democratic, liberal, and enlightened communism. Hungary cannot, of course, declare itself favorable toward Eurocommunism, since such a declaration would immediately bring on the flashes of the Soviet leaders. However, it has abstained as far as possible from turning its back to Eurocommunism and condemning it—as the Czechoslovak, East German, and Bulgarian parties have done several times following the example and orders received from Moscow. On December 7, 1976, during his visit to Vienna, János Kádár even declared at a press conference that "he did not share the view" that Eurocommunism would be anti-soviet.[4]

In the summer of 1977, in Rome, Kádár evaluated Eurocommunism and the experiment of the Italian Communist party even more favorably. As for the Hungarian press, it remains silent about the attacks of the fraternal parties against Berlinguer, Marchais, and Carillo, except for some comments of Soviet inspiration. If, on rare occasions, the Hungarian Communist party has yielded on this point to Moscow's pressure, it has not indulged in a noisy condemnation of Eurocommunism; it thereby shapes undeniable and valuable paths for its future development. Under present circumstances, the limits of this development are fixed by the Soviet power; however, with the help of favorable international circumstances, the HCP and Hungary itself could still make remarkable progress toward material well-being and freedom.

Notes

Chapter 1

1. Hereafter cited as HCP. The various names the HCP has given itself will be mentioned as they changed.

2. *A Magyar Munkásmozgalom történetének válogatott dokumentumai* [Selected documents on the history of the Hungarian workers' movement], vol. 5, November 7, 1917-March 21, 1919 (Budapest: Szikra, 1956), p. 351. Hereafter cited as *Selected documents*, vol. 5. See also György Milei, *A Kommunisták Magyarországi Pártjának megalakitásáról* [On the foundation of the Party of the Communists of Hungary] (Budapest: Kossuth, 1962).

3. *Munkásmozgalomtörténeti Lexikon* [Historical dictionary of the workers' movement] (Budapest: Kossuth, 1972). Hereafter cited as *Dictionary;* we refer to the items.

4. *Legyözhetetlen erö. A Magyar kommunista mozgalom szervezeti fejlödésének 50 éve* [Invincible force. Fifty years of evolution of the organization of the Hungarian communist movement] (Budapest: Kossuth, 1968). Hereafter cited as *Legyözhetetlen erö.*

5. *Selected documents*, vol. 5, pp. 311-12.

6. György Milei, "Mikor alakult a KP? [When was the C.P. founded?]" *Párttörténeti Közlemények* [Bulletin for Party History] 11, no. 3 (September 1965): 124-41. Hereafter cited as *PTK.*

7. On the Hungarian prisoners of war in Russia, see *Hadifogoly magyarok története. Második kötet: Az oroszországi hadifogság és a magyar hadifoglyok hazaszállitásának története* [History of the Hungarian prisoners of war, vol. 2, History of the Hungarian prisoners of war in Russia and their repatriation] (Budapest: Athenaeum, n.d.). On the group of communists, see *Selected documents*, vol. 5, pp. 97-120; *Dictionary*, s.v. "Ligeti," "Kun," "Szociális Forradalom," passim; as

149

well as "Dokumentumok as OK(b)P magyar csoportjának történetéböl, 1918-1919 [Documents relating to the history of the Hungarian group of the CP(b)R, 1918-1919]," *PTK* 4, no. 1 (January 1958): 165-89.

8. *Selected documents,* vol. 5, p. 118.

9. According to Sergei Lazo, 80-85 percent of the Red Army's foreign combatants were Hungarians. Ibid., p. 120. See also Antal Józsa and György Milei, *A rendithetetlen százezer Magyarok a nagy októberi szocialista forradalomban és a polgárháboruban* [The one hundred thousand resolute ones. Hungarians in the great socialist October revolution and in the civil war] (Budapest: Kossuth, 1968).

10. *Selected documents,* vol. 5, pp. 117-18; *PTK* 4, no. 1 (January 1958): 178.

11. Béla Kun, *A Magyar Tanácsköztársaságról* [On the Republic of the Councils of Hungary], selected speeches and writings (Budapest: Kossuth, 1958), p. 135.

12. *A magyar forradalmi munkásmozgalom története* [History of the revolutionary workers' movement of Hungary], vols. 1-2, 2d ed. (Budapest: Kossuth, 1970), p. 178. Hereafter cited as *History of the workers' movement.*

13. Vilmos Böhm, *Két forradalom tüzében* [In the fire of two revolutions] (Budapest: Népszava, 1946), p. 83.

14. We have consulted too many of the numerous sources and works on the events of 1918 to mention them here. For works of capital interest, we refer the reader to the writings of Count Mihály Károlyi, among which *Egy egész világ ellen* [Against an entire world] has gone through several editions. On the social democratic side, see Böhm, *Két forradalom tüzében.* On the radicals, see the memoirs of Oszkár Jászi, *Magyar kálvária, magyar feltámadás* [Hungarian calvary, Hungarian resurrection] (Vienna, 1920). A recent synthesis by Tibor Hajdu, *Az 1918—as magyarországi polgári demokratikus forradalom* [The democratic bourgeois revolution of Hungary in 1918] (Budapest: Kossuth, 1968). See also the general historical works in our bibliography.

15. Besides the sources and works indicated, see Mihály Károlyi, *Faith Without Illusions: The Memoirs of M. Károlyi* (London, 1956); Gyula Mérei, *A magyar oktoberi forradalom és a polgári pártok* [The Hungarian October revolution and the bourgeois parties] (Budapest: Akadémiai, 1969); Károly Mészáros, *Az öszirózsás forradalom és a Tanácsköztársaság parasztpolitikája* [The agrarian politics of the Queen Margaret revolution and of the Republic of the Councils] (Budapest: Akadémiai, 1966); Mihályné Károlyi, *Együtt a forradalomban* [Together in the revolution] (Budapest: Európa, 1967) (the memoirs

of Mrs. Károlyi).

16. Böhm, *Két forradalom tüzében*, pp. 79-80.

17. Ibid., p. 85.

18. See V. I. Lenin's article, "The attitude of the social democracy towards the peasant movement," published on September 14, 1905.

19. *Legyözhetetlen erö*, p. 17.

20. See, among others, the proclamations of the revolutionary socialists in *Selected documents*, vol. 5; as well as a letter of the writer Lajos Kassak from June 14, 1919, to Béla Kun (reproduced in *Action poétique*, no. 49 [Paris, 1972]).

21. We have translated this document according to a photographic reproduction of the text carrying also the signatures in *A magyar forradalmi munkásmozgalom története*, vols. 1-2 [History of the revolutionary workers' movement of Hungary], p. 219. In his memoirs, the former social democratic leader Vilmos Böhm gives a slightly different version of it, referring to a 1919 publication of the People's Commissariat for Public Education entitled *Az egység okmányai* [The documents of unity]. The most striking difference between the two versions is in the paragraph about the exercise of power. According to the photographic reproduction, "the representatives of the Party of the Communists of Hungary share *equally*" (or *also*—italics ours) in the leadership of the new party and political authority. The version quoted by Böhm reads: "the two parties jointly."

22. Károlyi, *Együtt a forradalomban*, pp. 466-67.

23. Böhm, *Két forradalom tüzében*, p. 292.

24. The sources and works relating to its history are also numerous. Besides the works and collections of documents mentioned in the text, some other titles are: *A Tanácsok országos gyülésének naplója* (1919 junius 14-1919 junius 23) [Proceedings of the National Assembly of the Councils, June 14, 1919-June 23, 1919] (Budapest: Athenaeum, 1919); *A Magyarországi Tanácsköztársaság 50. évfordulója* [Fiftieth anniversary of the Republic of the Councils of Hungary, transactions of the International Scientific Congress held in Budapest March 17-19, 1969] (Budapest: Akadémiai, 1970); Béláné Kun, *Kun Béla (Emlékezések)* [Béla Kun (recollections)] (Budapest: Magvetö, 1966); Gyula Hevesi, *Egy mérnök a forradalomban* [An engineer in the revolution] (Budapest: Európa, 1959); Ernö Garami, *Forrongó Magyarország* [Hungary in ferment] (Leipzig and Vienna, 1922).

25. *A Magyar Tanácsköztársaság pénzügyi rendszere* [The financial system of the Republic of the Councils of Hungary] (Budapest: Közgazdasági és jogi könyvkiadó, 1959), collection of essays published by Legal and Economic Editions.

26. *Történelmünk a jogalkotás tükrében* [Our history through legislation], collection of fundamental laws published by János Beér and Andor Csizmadia (Budapest: Gondolat, 1966).

27. Rudolf L. Tökés, *Béla Kun and the Hungarian Soviet Republic: The Origins and Role of the Communist Party of Hungary in the Revolutions of 1918-1919* (New York: Praeger, 1967), pp. 122-23.

28. Kun, *A Magyar Tanácsköztársaságról*, pp. 438-50.

29. Ibid.

30. *Papers Relating to the Foreign Relations of the United States. The Paris Peace Conference*, 13 vols. passim; Paul Mantoux, *Paris Peace Conference 1919*, Publications de l'Institut universitaire de hautes études internationales no. 43 (Geneva: Droz, 1964); Zsuzsa L. Nagy, *A párizsi békekonferencia és Magyarország* [The Paris Peace Conference and Hungary] (Budapest: Kossuth, 1965).

31. Branko Lazitch and Milorad M. Drachkovitch, *Lenin and the Comintern* (Stanford: Hoover Institution Press, 1972) 1: 110-24; Lucien Laurat, "Le Parti communiste autrichien," in *Contributions à l'histoire du Comintern* publiées sous la direction de Jacques Freymond, Publications de l'Institut universitaire de hautes études internationales no. 45 (Geneva: Droz, 1965); Sándorné Gábor, *Ausztria és a magyarországi tanácsköztársaság* [Austria and the Republic of the Councils of Hungary] (Budapest: Akadémai, 1969).

32. *Iratok az ellenforradalom történetéhez I. Az ellenforradalom hatalomrajutása és rémuralma Magyarországon 1919-1921* [Documents on the history of the counterrevolution. I. The accession to power and the terror of the counterrevolution in Hungary 1919-1921], published under the direction of Dezsö Nemes (Budapest: Szikra, 1956), passim.

33. *History of the Workers' Movement*, vols. 1-2, p. 291; see also *Hadifogoly magyarok története*, p. 567, which states that until December 1922, 137,989 prisoners of war returned from Russia to Hungary, including 1,584 who had until then been retained as hostages.

34. *History of the Workers' Movement*, vols. 1-2, p. 299. On the respective position of the leaders, see also Kun, *A Magyar Tanácsköztársaságról* as well as Jenö Landler, *Válogatott beszédek és irások* [Selected speeches and writings] (Budapest: Kossuth, 1960).

35. *PTK* 8, no. 2 (May 1962):1-34.

36. Ibid., no. 4 (November 1962):123-26.

37. *Legyözhetetlen erö*, p. 82; György Borsányi, "Adalékok a Kommunisták Magyarországi Pártja szervezeti fejlödéséhez, 1928-1932 [Facts relating to the development of the organization of the Party of the Communists of Hungary, 1928-1932]," *PTK* 8, no. 1 (March

1962): 46-75.

38. For the plenary session of 1928, see "Részletek a Kommunisták Magyarországi Pártja 1928 juliusi plénumának anyagából [Extracts from the documents of the plenary session of the Party of the Communists of Hungary in July 1928]," *PTK* 4, no. 3 (August 1958): 114-56. Georg Lukács participated in it under the pseudonym of Peterdi; his contributions to the debate still followed the general line of the HCP. For the Blum Theses, see "Részletek a 'Tézistertairól' (Blum-tézisek) cimü dokumentumból [Extracts from the document 'Thesis project on the Hungarian political and economic situation and on the tasks of the party' (Blum-Theses)],"*PTK* 2, no. 3 (October 1956): 75-94. See ibid., pp. 95-138, extracts from the "Discussion on the Blum-Theses" held in Budapest at the Petöfi Circle in 1956. Extensive extracts in German from the 1928 theses and from the 1956 debate can be found in Georg Lukács, *Schriften zur Ideologie und Politik* (Neuwied and Berlin: Luchterhand, 1967).

39. See the article by Borsányi in *PTK* 8, no. 1 (March 1962); as well as Zoltánné Horváth, "A Kommunisták Magyarországi Pártja II. kongreszszusa [The II. Congress of the Party of the Communists of Hungary]," *PTK* 9, no. 1 (February 1963): 37-41.

40. *Legyözhetetlen erö,* pp. 106-7; *History of the workers' movement,* pp. 437-39.

41. Besides *Legyözhetetlen erö* and *History of the workers' movement,* see Dezsö Orosz and István Pintér, "Adatok a KMP szervezeti fejlödéséhez, 1936-1942 [Facts on the evolution of the organization of the CP of Hungary, 1936-1942]," *PTK* 4, no. 3 (August 1958): 56-85, as well as János Kádár, "A Kommunisták Magyarországi Pártja feloszlatása korülményeinek és a Békepárt munkájának néhány kérdéséről, 1943 junius-1944 szeptember [Some questions concerning the circumstances of the dissolution of the Party of the Communists of Hungary and the activities of the Peace Party, June 1943-September 1944]," *PTK* 2, no. 3 (October 1956): 20-26.

42. *Legyözhetetlen erö,* pp. 108-9.

43. Lajos Papp, *Törvényenkivül* [Outlawed]. (Budapest: Kossuth, 1973), pp. 167-74.

44. Kádár, "A Kommunisták Magyarországi Pártja."

45. *A Magyar Tanácsköztársaság. A Kommunisták Magyarországi Pártjának harca a Horthy fasizmus ellen* [The Republic of the Councils of Hungary. The struggle of the Party of the Communists of Hungary against the Horthy fascism] (Budapest: Szikra, 1952), p. 45.

46. Gyula Kállai, *A magyar függetlenségi mozgalom, 1936-1945* [The Hungarian movement for independence, 1936-1945] (Budapest:

Kossuth, 1965), p. 78; *History of the workers' movement*, vols. 1-2, p. 451; István Pintér, *A magyar kommunisták a Hitler-ellenes nemzeti egységért, 1941 junius-1944 marcius* [Hungarian communists for anti-Hitlerian national unity, June 1941-March 1944] (Budapest: Kossuth, 1968). See also Gyula Kállai, *A Magyar Front és az ellenállás, 1944 marcius 19-1945 aprilis 4* [The Hungarian Front and resistance, March 19, 1944-April 4, 1945] (Budapest: Kossuth, 1970).

47. Endre Sik, *Vihar a levelet. . .* [Leaf in the storm . . .] (Budapest: Zrinyi, 1970); *Dictionary; Selected documents*, vols. 1-6; see also Branko Lazitch in collaboration with Milorad M. Drachkovitch, *Biographical Dictionary of the Comintern* (Stanford: Hoover Institution Press, 1973).

48. *Legyőzhetetlen erö*, p. 236.

49. According to official figures, seventeen persons in all have been expelled from the party for having participated in the "illegal proceedings" of the Stalinist era and six others for having conspired with Rákosi and Gerö. See *A Magyar Szocialista Munkáspárt Központi Bizottságának határozata a személyi kultusz éveiben a munkásmozgalmi emberek ellen inditott törvénysértö perek lezárásáró* (pamphlet 16VIII62) [Resolution of the Central Committee of the Hungarian Socialist Workers' Party on the closure of the illegal trials brought against militants of the workers' movement during the years of the personality cult] (Budapest: Kossuth, 1962).

50. *A Magyar Szocialista Munkáspárt Központi Bizottságának kongresszusi irányelvei* [Instructions of the Central Committee of the Hungarian Socialist Workers' Party for the congress] (Budapest: Kossuth, 1962), pp. 39-49.

51. Speech published exclusively in the *New Hungarian Quarterly* 13, no. 48 (Budapest, 1972).

52. *A Magyar Szocialiste Munkáspárt XI. kongresszusának jegyzökönyve 1975. marcius 17-22* [Proceedings of the XI. Congress of the Hungarian Socialist Workers' Party] (Budapest: Kossuth Könyvkiado, 1975).

Chapter 2

1. Besides Böhm's work, see Árpád Szélpál, *Les 133 jours de Béla Kun* (Paris: Fayard, 1959), p. 158.

2. We have drawn all this statistical data from the official publication *Legyőzhetetlen erö*, except for the last total, which results from our addition (instead of the figure 880,717 furnished in the cited source).

3. *Legyőzhetetlen erö*, p. 197.

4. Besides *Legyözhetetlen erö,* cf. *A Magyar Szocialista Munkáspárt IX. kongresszusának jegyzökönyve* [Proceedings of the IX. Congress of the Hungarian Socialist Workers' Party] (Budapest: Kossuth, 1967).

5. *Legyözhetetlen erö,* p. 243; it is not indicated whether the 30.3 percent figure, like the preceding ones, is obtained from the industrial statistics or from the new calculation of the professional percentages. See the text for our interpretation of this figure as well as note 7 in this chapter.

6. Ibid., p. 243.

7. In fact, we have ourselves transposed this figure of 30.3 percent to table 3; see note 5 in this chapter.

8. *Proceedings of the IX. Congress,* p. 117.

9. Contrary to the majority of the Muscovites, the four have been spared during the purges. We shall come back to this point.

10. See the unpublished thesis of Dominique Gros, "Les Conseils ouvriers, espérances et défaites de la révolution en Autriche-Hongrie 1917-1920," University of Dijon.

11. Ágnes Ságvári, *Népfront és koalició Magyarországon 1936-1948* [Popular front and coalition in Hungary 1936-1948] (Budapest: Kossuth, 1967), pp. 118-21.

12. Béla Balázs, "A nemzeti bizottságok szerepe népi demokráciánk létrejöttében [The role of the national committees in the formation of our people's democracy]," in *Tanulmányok a magyar népi demokrácia történetéböl* [Studies concerning the history of the Hungarian people's democracy], under the direction of Miklós Lackó (Budapest: Akadémiai, 1955).

13. Miklós Molnár, *Budapest 1956. A History of the Hungarian Revolution* (London: George Allen and Unwin, 1971), pp. 174-80, 246-50.

Chapter 3

1. Paul Lendvai, *L'Antisémitisme sans juifs* (Paris: Fayard, 1971), pp. 34, 321, 347.

2. Ferenc Donáth, *Demokratikus földreform Magyarországon 1945-1947* [Democratic land reform in Hungary 1945-1947] (Budapest; Akadémiai, 1969); *A népi Magyarország negyedszázada* [A quarter of a century of people's democracy in Hungary], transactions of the international scientific session on the occasion of the twenty-fifth anniversary of the liberation of Hungary (Budapest: Akadémiai, 1972).

3. *Képes politikai és gazdasági világatlasz* [Illustrated political and economic world atlas] (Budapest: Kartográfiai vállalat, 1966); *Magyar*

statisztikai Zsebkönyv [Statistical handbook of Hungary] (Budapest: Statisztikai kiadi, 1975).

4. *A népi Magyarország negyedszázada*, pp. 35-37; *L'Europe de l'Est en 1970*, étude réalisée par Thomas Schreiber. La documentation française. Notes et études documentaires. Nos. 3,781-3,782-3,783 (Paris, 1971). For the per capita national income, see Stark Antal, Gazdaságunk szerkezetéröl," *Valósag* 20, no. 9 (September 1977).

5. *Társadalmi rétegzödés Magyarországon* [Social stratification in Hungary], study published under the direction of Mrs. Aladár Mód (Budapest: Central Office for Statistics, 1966).

6. The expression in quotes is actually untranslatable because the adjective *uri* is derived from *ur*, which means at the same time lord, gentleman, and master.

7. Emil Gulyás, "A magyar mezögazdaság fejlödése nemzetközi összehasonlitasban mezögasdaságunk szocialista átszervezése óta [The development of Hungarian agriculture since its socialist transformation as compared international study]," in *A népi Magyarország negyedszázada*, p. 367. See also in the same volume Sándor Orbán, "A parasztság osztálytagozódásának alakulása a felszabadulás után [Evolution of the social stratification of the peasantry since the liberation]," pp. 335-46, as well as by the same author, *Két agrárforradalom Magyarországon. Demokratikus és szocialista agrárátalakulás 1945-1961* [Two agrarian revolutions in Hungary. Democratic and socialist agrarian transformations 1945-1961] (Budapest: Akadémiai, 1972). See also *Statistical handbook* (1975).

8. Molnár, *Budapest 1956*, p. 182.

9. François Fejtö, *L'Héritage de Lénine* (Paris: Casterman, 1973), p. 96.

10. *History of the workers' movement*, vols. 1-2, p. 438.

11. See the collection of essays *A Kommunista Párt szövetségi politikája 1936-1962* [The policy of alliances of the Communist Party 1936-1962] (Budapest: Kossuth, 1966).

12. Ságvári, *Népfront és koalició Magyarországon 1936-1948*, p. 35.

13. For a different view, see above p. 40, the extract of a work by Gyula Kállai.

14. The Central Committee Abroad addresses itself to the Committee of the interior. Cf. above.

15. *Dokumentumok a magyar párttörténet tanulmányozásához* [Documents for the study of the history of the Hungarian party] (Budapest: Szikra, 1955) 5: 58-60.

16. See ibid., footnote of the editors: "So far we have not re-

covered the documents in question.''

17. See among others Georg Lukács, *Schriften zur Literatursoziologie* (Neuwied and Berlin: Luchterhand, 1970). See also Tamás Aczél and Tibor Méray, *The Revolt of the Mind* (New York: Praeger, 1959) as well as Molnár, *Budapest 1956.*

18. See especially the memoirs of the Hungarian statesmen who were exiled or sought refuge in the West: Ferenc Nagy, Imre Kovács, Dezsö Sulyok.

19. *History of the workers' movement,* vol. 3, pp. 197-98.

20. William O. McCagg, "Communism and Hungary, 1944-1945," (Ph.D. diss., Columbia University, 1964). See also Yehuda Lahav, *The Hungarian Communist Party's Path to Power 1944-1948,* Ph.D. diss., Hebrew University, Jerusalem, 1976 (English abstract).

21. Vincent Savarius, *Minden kényszer nélkül* [Volunteers for the gallows] (Brussels: Nagy Imre Intezet, 1963); Tibor Méray, *Thirteen Days that shook the Kremlin* (New York: Praeger, 1959).

Chapter 4

1. *L'Affaire Rajk,* compte rendu sténographique complet des séances du Tribunal du Peuple à Budapest, du 16 au 24 septembre 1949 (Paris: Les Editeurs français réunis, 1949), p. 389.

2. See Nikita S. Khrouchtchev, *Souvenirs* (Paris: Laffont, 1971); as well as the examination of various pieces of information on Belgrade's attitude in Molnár, *Budapest 1956.*

3. Sik, *Vihar a levelet . . . ; Dictionary.*

Chapter 5

1. They belong to the total of fifty-three Hungarian victims whom we were able to identify. See above, chap. 4, p. 132.

2. Annie Kriegel: *Les communistes français,* 2d ed. (Paris, Seuie 1970).

3. *History of the workers' movement,* vol. 3, p. 197.

4. See the *Corriere della Sera,* and other newspapers which reported the event, as well as a declaration of Kádár in the *New Hungarian Quarterly* 33, no. 66 (Summer 1977).

Bibliography

Primary Sources

L'Affaire Rajk. Compte rendu sténographique complet des séances du Tribunal du Peuple à Budapest, du 16 au 24 septembre 1949. Paris: Les Editeurs Français Réunis, 1949.

Böhm, Vilmos. *Két forradalom tüzében* [In the fire of two revolutions]. Budapest: Népszava, 1946.

Dokumentumok a magyar párttörténet tanulmányozásához. IV. 1929 októberétöl-1939 szeptemberéig. V. 1939 szeptemberétöl-1945 áprilisáig. [Documents for the study of the history of the Hungarian party: vol. 4. October 1929-September 1939; vol. 5. September 1939-April 1945.] Budapest: Szikra, 1955.

Földreform 1945. Tanulmány és dokumentumgyüjtemény. Levéltárak országos központja és a MTA Történettudományi intézete. [Land reform 1945. Study and collection of documents. National Center of Archives and Institute for historical sciences of the Hungarian Academy of Sciences]. Budapest: Kossuth, 1965.

Garami, Ernö. *Forrongó Magyarország* [Hungary in ferment]. Leipzig and Vienna, 1922.

Hevesi, Gyula. *Egy mérnök a forradalomban* [An engineer in the revolution]. Budapest: Európa, 1959.

Illés, Béla. *Eg a Tisza* [The Tisza in flames]. Budapest: Szépirodalmi, 1966.

Iratok az ellenforradalom történetéhez. I. As ellenforradalom hatalomrajutása és rémuralma Magyarországon 1919-1921. [Documents on the history of the counterrevolution. Vol. 1. The accession to power and the terror of the counterrevolution in Hungary 1919-1921]. Published under the direction of Dezsö Nemes. Budapest: Szikra, 1956.

Kádár, János. "Reflections at sixty." *The New Hungarian Quarterly* 13, no. 48 (Budapest, winter 1972): 5-14.

——. *A szocialista Magyarországért. Beszédek és cikkek, 1968-1972* [For a socialist Hungary. Speeches and writings]. Budapest: Kossuth, 1972.

Károlyi, Mihály. *Egy egész világ ellen* [Against an entire world]. Munich: Verlag für Kulturpolitik, 1923.

——. *Faith Without Illusions: Memoirs of Michael Karolyi.* London: Cape, 1956.

Károlyi, Mihályné. *Együtt a forradalomban* [Together in the revolution]. Budapest: Európa, 1967.

Keresztes, Mihály. *Az elsö lépések* [The first steps]. Budapest: Kossuth, 1971.

Khrouchtchev, Nikita S. *Souvenirs.* Paris: Laffont, 1971.

Kiss, Károly. *Nincs megállás* [No stoppage]. Budapest: Kossuth, 1974.

Kovács, Imre. *Im Schatten der Sovjets.* Zürich: Thomas Verlag, 1948.

Kun, Béla. *A Magyar Tanácsköztársaságról* [On the Republic of the Councils of Hungary]. Selected speeches and writings. Budapest: Kossuth, 1958.

Kun, Béláné. *Kun Béla (Emlékezések)* [Béla Kun (Recollections)]. Budapest: Magvetö, 1966.

Landler, Jenö. *Válogatott beszédek és irások* [Selected speeches and writings]. Budapest: Kossuth, 1960.

Lengyel, József. *Elévült tartozás* [Remitted Debt]. Budapest: Szépirodalmi, 1964.

——. "Visegrádi utca" [Visegrad Street]. In *Mérni a mérhetetlent* [Measuring the immeasurable]. Vol. 2, pp. 7-200. Budapest: Szépirodalmi, 1966.

Lénine, V. I. "L'attitude de la social-démocratie à l'égard du mouvement paysan." In *Oeuvres choisies.* Vol 1, pp. 534-42. Moscow: Editions en langues étrangères, 1948.

Lukács, Georg. *Schriften zur Ideologie und Politik.* Neuwied and Berlin: Luchterhand, 1967.

——. *Schriften zur Literatursoziologie.* Neuwied and Berlin: Luchterhand, 1970.

A Magyar Dolgozók Pártja II. kongresszusának határozata [Resolution of the II. Congress of the Hungarian Workers' Party]. Kiadja a MDP KV [Edited by the Central Committee of the Hungarian Workers' Party]. N.d., n.p.

A Magyar Kommunista Párt és a Szociáldemokrata Párt határozatai 1944-1948 [Resolutions of the Hungarian Communist Party and of the Social Democratic Party 1944-1948]. Budapest: Kossuth, 1967.

A Magyar Kommunista Párt IV. Kongresszusa (1948 jùnius 12); A Szo-

ciáldemokrata Párt XXXVII. Kongresszusa (1948 jùnius 12); A Magyar Kommunista Párt és a Szociáldemokrata Párt Egyesülési Kongresszusa jegyzökönyve (1948 jùnius 12-13-14) [Proceedings of the IV. Congress of the Hungarian Communist Party (June 12, 1948); of the XXXVII. Congress of the Social Democratic Party (June 12, 1948); of the congress for the union of the Hungarian Communist Party and the Social Democratic Party (June 12-13-14, 1948)]. Budapest: Szikra, 1956.

A Magyar Munkásmozgalom történetének válogatott dokumentumai [Selected documents on the history of the Hungarian workers' movement]. Vol. 5 (November 7, 1917-March 21, 1919). Budapest: Szikra, 1956.

Magyar Statisztileai Zsebkönyv 1975. [Hungarian Statistical Handbook 1975]. Budapest: Közpouti Statisztikai Hivatal [Central Statistical Office] —Statisztikai Kiadó, 1975.

A Magyar Szocialista Munkáspárt IX. kongresszusának jegyzökönyve [Proceedings of the IX. Congress of the Hungarian Socialist Workers' Party]. Budapest: Kossuth, 1967.

Magyar Szocialista Munkáspárt X. kongresszusának jegyzökönyve (1970 november 23-28) [Proceedings of the X. Congress of the Hungarian Socialist Workers' Party (November 23-28, 1970)]. Budapest: Kossuth, 1971.

A Magyar Szocialista Munkáspárt XI. kongresszusának jegyzökönyve 1975. marcius 17-22 [Proceedings of the XI. Congress of the Hungarian Socialist Workers' Party, March 17-22, 1975]. Budapest: Kossuth, 1975.

A Magyar Szocialista Munkáspárt Központi Bizottságának kongresszusi irányelvei. A Magyar Szocialista Munkáspárt Központi Bizottságának határozata a személyi kultusz éveiben a munkásmozgalmi emberek ellen inditott törvénysértö perek lezárásáról [Instructions of the Central Committee of the Hungarian Socialist Workers' Party for the congress. Resolution of the Central Committee of the Hungarian Socialist Workers' Party on the closure of the illegal trials brought against militants of the workers' movement during the years of the personality cult]. Budapest: Kossuth, 1962.

Mantoux, Paul. *Paris Peace Conference 1919.* Publications de l'Institut universitaire de hautes études internationales no. 43. Geneva: Droz, 1964.

Marosán, György. *Az ùton végig kell menni* [The road must be traveled]. Budapest: Magvetö zsebkönyvtar, 1972.

Nagy, Ferenc. *The Struggle behind the Iron Curtain.* New York: Macmillan, 1948.

——. *Ahogy én láttam*... [As I saw it ...]. Budapest: Gondolat, 1965.

Nagy, Imre. *Egy évtized. Válogatott beszédek és irások* [A decade. Selected speeches and writings]. Budapest: Szikra, 1954.

Nagy, Vince. *Octóbertöl-októberig. Emlékiratok-önéletrajz* [From October to October. Recollections/autobiography]. New York: Pro Arte Publishing Co., 1962.

Nógrádi, Sándor. *Avant 1956. Chronique hongroise.* Paris: Eds. du Pavillon, 1969.

——. *Történelmi lecke* [Historical lesson]. Budapest: Kossuth, 1970.

——. *Uj történet kezdödött* [A new history has begun]. Budapest: Kossuth, 1966.

Olvasókönyv a magyar és a nemzetközi munkásmozgalom történetének tanulmányozásához 1945-1969 [Reading book for the study of the history of the Hungarian and international workers' movement 1945-1969]. Budapest: Kossuth, 1969-1970.

Papers relating to the Foreign Relations of the United States. The Paris Peace Conference. 13 vols. Washington, D.C.: U.S. Government Printing Office, 1942-47.

Papp, Lajos. *Törvényen kivül* [Outlawed]. Budapest: Kossuth, 1973.

Rákosi, Mátyás. *Válogatott beszédek és cikkek* [Selected speeches and articles]. Budapest: Szikra, 1955.

Révai, Yózsef. *Literarische Studien.* Berlin: Dietz, 1956.

Romanelli, Guido. *Nell'Ungheria di Bela Kun e durante l'occupazione militare romena. La mia missione maggio-novembre 1919.* Udine: Doretti, 1964.

Rudas, László. *Abenteurer und Liquidatoren. Die Politik Béla Kuns und die Krise der KPU.* Wien, 1922.

Savarius, Vincent [Szasz, Bela]. *Minden kényszer nélkül* [Volunteers for the gallows]. Brussels: Nagy Imre Intézet [Imre Nagy Institute], 1963.

Sik, Endre. *Vihar a levelet*... [Leaf in the storm ...]. Budapest: Zrinyi, 1970.

Sulyok, Desiderius. *Zwei Nächte ohne Tag.* Zürich: Thomas Verlag, 1948.

Szamuely, Tibor. *Összegyüjtött irások és beszédek* [Collected writings and speeches]. Budapest: Magvetö, 1975.

Szekér, Nándor. *Föld alatt és föld felett* [Dead and alive]. Budapest: Kossuth, 1968.

A tanácsok országos gyülésének (1919 junius 14-1919 junius 23) Naplója. A munkás és katonatanácsok gyorsirodájának feljegyzései alapján [Proceedings of the National Assembly of the Councils (June 14, 1919-June 23, 1919)]. Based on the notes of the stenographic bureau of the workers' and soldiers' councils. Budapest: Athenaeum r.t., 1919.

Történelmünk a jogalkotás tükrében [Our history through legislation]. Collection of fundamental laws published by János Beér and Andor Csizmadia. Budapest: Gondolat, 1966.

Vas, Zoltán. *Hazatérés, 1944* [Return, 1944]. Budapest: Szépirodalmi, 1970.

Zamercev, I.T. *Emlékek, arcok, Budapest... Egy szovjet városparancsnok visszaemlékezései* [Recollections, faces, Budapest... Recollections of a Soviet governor]. Translated from Russian. Budapest: Zrinyi, 1969.

Books

Aczél, Tamás, and Méray, Tibor. *The Revolt of the Mind. A Case History of Intellectual Resistance behind the Iron Curtain.* New York: Praeger, 1959.

Bibó, István. *Harmadik út. Politikai és történeti tanylmányok* [The third way. Political and historical essays]. With an introduction by Zoltán Szabó. London: Magyar könyves céh, 1960.

Berecz, János. *Ellenforradalom tollal és fegyverrel 1956* [Counterrevolution through the pen and through arms 1956]. Budapest: Kossuth, 1969.

Csatari, Dániel. *Forgó szélben (Magyar-román viszony 1940-1945)* [In shifting winds (Hungarian-Rumanian relations 1940-1945)]. Budapest: Akadémiai, 1968.

Donáth, Ferenc. *Demokratikus földreform Magyarországon 1945-1947* [Democratic land reform in Hungary 1945-1947]. Budapest: Akadémiai, 1969.

Fejtö, François. *Dictionnaire des partis communistes et des mouvements révolutionnaires.* Précédé d'un essai sur la crise actuelle de l'internationalisme marxiste. Paris: Casterman, 1971.

———. *L'Héritage de Lénine.* Paris: Casterman, 1973.

Fukász, György. *A magyarországi polgári radikalizmus történetéhez, 1900-1918. Jászi Oszkár ideológiájának birálata* [Contribution to the history of bourgeois radicalism in Hungary, 1900-1918. A critique of Oszkár Jászi's ideology]. Budapest: Gondolat, 1960.

Gábor, Sándorné. *Ausztria és a magyarországi tanácsköztársaság* [Austria and the Republic of the Councils of Hungary]. Budapest: Akadémiai, 1969.

Gosztonyi, Péter. *Die ungarische antifaschistische Bewegung in der*

Sowjetunion während des Zweiten Weltkrieges. Sonderdruck aus Militärgeschichtliche Mitteilungen 1/1972. Karlsruhe: Verlag G. Braun, 1972.

Gros, Dominique. "Les Conseils ouvriers, espérances et défaites de la révolution en Autriche-Hongrie 1917-1920." Thesis, University of Dijon, 1973.

Hadifogoly magyarok története. Második kötet: Az oroszországi hadifogság és a magyar hadifoglyok hazaszállitásának története [History of the Hungarian prisoners of war. Vol. 2. History of the Hungarian prisoners of war in Russia and their repatriation]. Budapest: Athenaeum, n.d.

Hajdu, Tibor. *Az 1918—as magyarországi polgári demokratikus forradalom* [The democratic bourgeois revolution of Hungary in 1918]. Budapest: Kossuth, 1968.

——. *A Magyarországi Tanács-Köztársaság* [The Hungarian Soviet Republic]. Budapest: Kossuth, 1969.

Horváth, Zoltán. *Die Jahrhundertwende in Ungarn. Geschichte der zweiten Reformgeneration (1896-1914).* Budapest: Corvina Verlag, 1966.

Horváth, Zoltánné. *A KMP második kongresszusa* [The second congress of the Hungarian Party of the Communists]. Budapest: Kossuth, 1964.

Ignotus, Paul. *Hungary.* London: Ernest Benn, 1972.

Jászi, Oszkár. *Magyar kalvária, magyar feltámadás* [Hungarian calvary, Hungarian resurrection]. Vienna, 1920.

Józsa, Antal, and Milei, György. *A rendithetlen százezer. Magyarok a nagy októberi szocialista forradalomban és a polgárháborúban* [The one hundred thousand resolute ones. Hungarians in the great socialist October revolution and in the civil war]. Budapest: Kossuth, 1968.

Kállai, Gyula. *A magyar függetlenségi mozgalom 1936-1945* [The Hungarian movement for independence 1936-1945]. Budapest: Kossuth, 1965.

Képes politikai és gazdasági világatlasz [Illustrated political and economic world atlas]. Budapest: Kartográfiai vállalat, 1966.

Kiss, Artùr. *Az "új osztály"—fantázia vagy valóság?* [The "new class"—fantasy or reality?]. Budapest: Kossuth, 1971.

A Kommunista Párt szövetségi politikája 1936-1962 [The policy of alliances of the Communist Party 1936-1962]. Budapest: Kossuth, 1966.

Kriegel, Annie. *Les Communistes français.* Paris: Seuil, 1970.

Lackó, Miklós. *Válságok—választások* [Crisis—alternatives]. Budapest:

Gondolat, 1975.

Laurat, Lucien. "Le Parti communiste autrichien." In *Contributions à l'histoire du Comintern* publiées sous la direction de Jacques Freymond. Publications de l'Institut universitaire de hautes études internationales no. 45. Geneva: Droz, 1965.

Lazitch, Branko, in collaboration with Drachkovitch, Milorad M. *Biographical Dictionary of the Comintern*. Stanford: Hoover Institution Press, 1973.

Lazitch, Branko, and Drachkovitch, Milorad M. *Lenin and the Comintern*. Stanford: Hoover Institution Press, 1972.

Legyözhetetlen erö. A magyar kommunista mozgalom szervezeti fejlödésének 50 éve [Invincible force. Fifty years of evolution of the organization of the Hungarian communist movement]. Budapest: Kossuth, 1968.

Lendvai, Paul. *L'Antisémitisme sans juifs*. Paris: Fayard, 1971.

McCagg, William O. "Communism and Hungary, 1944-1945." Ph.D. diss., Columbia University, 1964.

A magyar forradalmi munkásmozgalom története [History of the revolutionary workers' movement of Hungary]. Vols. 1-3. 2d ed. Budapest: Kossuth, 1970.

Magyar önkéntesek a spanyol nép szabadságharcában [Hungarian volunteers in the struggle for freedom of the Spanish people.]. Budapest: Kossuth, 1959.

A Magyar Tanácsköztársaság. A Kommunisták Magyarországi Pártjának harca a Horthy-fasizmus ellen [The Republic of the Councils of Hungary. The struggle of the Party of the Communists of Hungary against the Horthy fascism]. Budapest: Szikra, 1962.

Magyarország Története 1918-1919, 1919-1945 [History of Hungary 1918-1919, 1919-1945]. Budapest: Akadémiai, 1976.

A Magyarországi Tanácsköztársaság 50. évfordulója. Nemzetközi tudományos ülésszak (Budapest, 1969 március 17-19) [Fiftieth anniversary of the Republic of the Councils of Hungary. Transactions of the international scientific congress held in Budapest March 17-19, 1969]. Budapest: Akadémiai, 1970.

A Magyar Tanácsköztársaság pénzügyi rendszere [The financial system of the Republic of the Councils of Hungary]. Collection of essays published by Legal and Economic Editions. Budapest: Közgazdasági és jogi könyvkiadó, 1959.

Méray, Tibor. *Thirteen Days that shook the Kremlin*. New York: Praeger, 1959.

Mérei, Gyula. *A magyar októberi forradalom és a polgári pártok* [The Hungarian October revolution and the bourgeois parties]. Budapest: Akadémiai, 1969.

Mészáros, Károly. *Az öszirózsás forradalom és a Tanácsköztársaság parasztpolitikája* [The agrarian politics of the Queen Margaret revolution and of the Republic of the Councils.]. Budapest: Akadémiai, 1966.

Milei, György. *A Kommunisták Magyarországi Pártjának megalakitásáról* [On the foundation of the Party of the Communists of Hungary]. Budapest: Kossuth, 1962.

Molnár, Miklós. *Budapest 1956. A History of the Hungarian Revolution.* London: George Allen and Unwin, 1971.

——. "Révolution, contre-révolution et politique étrangère: Hongrie 1919." *Relations Internationales* (Geneva), 1975, no. 4.

Munkásmozgalomtörténeti Lexikon [Historical dictionary of the workers' movement]. Budapest: Kossuth, 1972.

Nagy, Zsuzsa L. *A párizsi békekonferencia és Magyarország* [The Paris Peace Conference and Hungary]. Budapest: Kossuth, 1965.

Nemes, Dezsö. *Magyarország felszabadulása.* Magyarország fejlödése a felszabadulás után [The liberation of Hungary. The development of Hungary after the liberation]. Budapest: Kossuth, 1960.

A népi Magyarország negyedszázada [A quarter of a century of people's democracy in Hungary]. Transactions of the international scientific session on the occasion of the twenty-fifth anniversary of the liberation of Hungary. Budapest: Akadémiai, 1972.

Orbán, Sándor. *Két agrárforradalom Magyarországon. Demokratikus és szocialista agrárátalakulás 1945-1961* [Two agrarian revolutions in Hungary. Democratic and socialist agrarian transformations 1945-1961]. Budapest: Akadémiai, 1962.

A pártélet és a pártmunka idöszerü kérdései [Current questions on party life and work]. Budapest: Kossuth, 1973.

Pintér, István. *A Magyar Front és az ellenállás (1944 március 19-1945 április 4)* [The Hungarian Front and resistance (March 19, 1944-April 4, 1945)]. Budapest: Kossuth, 1970.

——. *A magyar kommunisták a Hitler-ellenes nemzeti egységért. 1941 június-1944 március* [Hungarian communists for anti-Hitlerian national unity. June 1941-March 1944]. Budapest: Kossuth, 1968.

Puskás, A. I. *Magyarország a II. világháborúban* [Hungary in World War II]. Translated from Russian. Abridged version. Budapest: Kossuth, 1971.

Ságvári, Agnes. *Népfront és koalició Magyarországon 1936-1948* [Popular front and coalition in Hungary 1936-1948]. Budapest:Kossuth, 1967.

Schöpflin, Byula. "Dokumentum. A Magyar Kommunista Párt ùtja,

1945-1950 [Document. The path of the Hungarian Communist Party, 1945-1950]." In *Látóhatár.* Munich, 1955.

Schreiber, Thomas, *L'Europe de l'Est en 1970.* La documentation française. Notes et études documentaires. Nos. 3,781-3,783. Paris, 1971.

The Soviet Union and Eastern Europe: A Handbook. Edited by George Schöpflin. London: Anthony Blond, 1970.

A szabadság vértanui. Az életrajzokat irta: T. Szerémi Borbála. A Magyar Szocialista Munkáspárt Központi Bizottságának Párttörténeti intézete [The martyrs of freedom. Biographies by T. Szerémi Borbála. Institute for Party History of the Central Committee of the Hungarian Socialist Workers' Party]. Budapest: Kossuth, 1960.

Szabó, Ágnes. *A Kommunisták Magyarországi Pártjának ujraszervezése (1919-1925)* [The reorganization of the Hungarian Party of the Communists (1919-1925)]. Budapest: Kossuth, 1970.

Szamuely, Tibor. *A Kommunisták Magyarországi Pártjának unegalakulása, és harca a proletárdiktaturáért* [The founding of the Party of the Communists of Hungary and its fight for the proletarian dictatorship]. Budapest: Kossuth, 1964.

Szépál, Árpád. *Les 133 jours de Béla Kun.* Paris: Fayard, 1959.

Szenes, Iván. *A Kommunista Párt Ujjástervetése Magyarországon 1956-1957.* [The Reorganization of the Communist Party in Hungary 1956-1957]. Budapest: Kossuth, 1976.

Tanulmányok a magyar népi demokrácia történetéböl [Studies concerning the history of the Hungarian people's democracy]. Under the direction of Miklós Lackó. Budapest: Akadémiai, 1955.

Társadalmi rétegezödés Magyarországon [Social stratification in Hungary]. Study published under the direction of Mrs. Aladár Mód. Budapest: Central Office for Statistics, 1966.

Tökés, Rudolf L. *Béla Kun and the Hungarian Soviet Republic: The Origins and Role of the Communist Party of Hungary in the Revolutions of 1918-1919.* New York and Washington: Praeger, 1967.

Vadász, Ferenc. *Tenyérnyi ég* [A patch of blue]. Budapest: Kossuth, 1970.

Periodicals

Szabad Nép [Free People]. Daily of the HCP. Budapest 1945-1946.

Népszabadság [Freedom of the People]. Daily of the HCP. Budapest 1956-1977.

Párttörténeti Közlemények [Bulletin for Party History]. Historical review of the Institute for Party History of the Central Committee of the Hungarian Socialist Workers' Party. Budapest 1955-1977.

Társadalmi Szemle [Social Review]. Theoretical and political review of
the CP. Budapest 1945-1975.
Valóság [Reality]. Budapest 1957-1977.